A Manifesto for Excellence in Schools

Rob Carpenter

BLOOMSBURY EDUCATION

LONDON OXFORD NEW YORK NEW DELHI SYDNEY

BLOOMSBURY EDUCATION
Bloomsbury Publishing Plc
50 Bedford Square, London, WC1B 3DP, UK

BLOOMSBURY, BLOOMSBURY EDUCATION and the Diana logo are trademarks of
Bloomsbury Publishing Plc

First published in Great Britain 2018 by Bloomsbury Publishing Plc

A catalogue record for this book is available from the British Library

ISBN: PB: 978-1-4729-4634-8; ePDF: 978-1-4729-4632-4; ePub: 978-1-4729-4633-1

2 4 6 8 10 9 7 5 3 1

Typeset by Newgen KnowledgeWorks Pvt. Ltd., Chennai, India
Printed and bound in India by Replika Press Pvt. Ltd.

All papers used by Bloomsbury Publishing Plc are natural, recyclable products from
wood grown in well managed forests. The manufacturing processes conform to the
environmental regulations of the country of origin

To find out more about our authors and books visit www.bloomsbury.com
and sign up for our newsletters

11/18

A N

Exc

This book is dedicated to my nan,
Mrs Elsie Flitcroft.
Every child needs a champion and she was mine.

CONTENTS

Preface

By the age of seven, I had already attended five different schools, moved house four times and been taught by six different teachers – that number rose to ten teachers before I finished my primary education. Hopping between different schools, I developed an acute awareness about what made schools good or not. This was based primarily on subjective experiences – who I was sat next to, relationships with teachers – and environmental factors, such as the smells of the school, how warm the milk was, colours on the walls and quality of the reading books we were given. These intimate associations between environment and senses were an early indicator that shaped my beliefs about the impact school climate has in regulating the temperature of how we feel. Essentially, I was beginning to form a nucleus of understanding about what determines whether a school is warm, welcoming and open to learning – or not.

At ten years old, I knew that Mrs Jose favoured certain children and that whatever I did to win her approval was never going to be enough. I learnt that some teachers were fair, while others were not. I knew which staff were more compassionate and those who had a tendency to abuse their privilege. I knew that Mrs Lewis, the dinner lady, genuinely loved children and did not resent turning the skipping rope in all weathers, because she liked to make kids feel good about themselves. Finally, I understood that Mr Bounds and Mrs Ainscough believed in me – more than that, they championed me – whereas the school secretary didn't. Thank you, Mr Bounds and Mrs Ainscough.

The shame of being a 'free school meals kid' will always remain with me. It was painfully reinforced by the daily ritual of announcing, during registration, that I was 'free dinners', before collecting a token that I was made to hang on a peg inside the school office. It's funny what you remember about school and the impact this has.

There were three key lessons I learnt from these early childhood encounters with formal education:

1   A school is only as good as the relationships it fosters and the way these are enshrined in the behaviours of each individual.

2   All schools carry biases, preferences and blind spots to their own weaknesses, even if they don't know they do.

3   In the end, all that matters is how we *feel* about the places we spend most of our time in. It is the sense of belonging that defines our experiences.

There was a fourth lesson I have just learnt from retelling this part of my story: schools should listen to children more, especially those who are more vulnerable than others.

The aim of this book is to help teachers, school leaders and policymakers re-evaluate what makes the biggest difference to the lives of children in schools, reframing the narrative of school improvement so that we understand better how lasting change is driven – not by individuals or prescriptive accountability frameworks, but by enduring relationships that place children at the centre of all we do. We have, over the years, made education an increasingly complex business, finding ever more scientific or objective ways to evaluate learning and justify decision-making. Policy development has become more centralised; we employ more people now to service the system rather than improve the system, and we have built an entire accountability framework to compensate for a lack of faith in teachers to regulate the culture and climate within the walls of our classrooms.

Ironically, many of the challenges we face in education have been created by the complex interventions meant to solve the problems in the first place! The simplicity of education and learning has been swept away by PISA league tables (Programme for International Student Assessment), strategy, efficiency and just about anything that distracts us from our core focus: building a legacy of positive, affirming relationships where children flourish, making powerful connections between learning and its bigger cause – to transform lives and communities. Just as you don't need to perform brain surgery every time someone bumps their head, nor have we needed pseudo-scientific education strategies that overcomplicate what we know already about the most important thing in schools: relationships. In other words, the wisdom and experience that we need to create a better education future already sits in our schools and is worth more than intellectual, academic theory.

Introduction

Lessons from headteacher interviews

I took on my first headteacher role at Bannockburn Primary School in Plumstead, South East London, in 2003. My interview for the position involved important learning that I want to share with you now. As part of the recruitment process, I was invited to deliver an assembly, and I obliged with the 'long spoons' activity, which was meant to demonstrate the value of collaboration. The aim was for me to narrate an impressive tale about geese honking support to each other, flying in collective formation and generally working as a team in order to get from one place to the next. The grand finale would consist of two carefully selected pupils from the assembly group feeding each other fruit pieces using impossibly long spoons (made by skilfully sticky taping bamboo canes to one end of a normal spoon), thus making it too difficult for the children to feed themselves. The moral of the assembly: we, like geese, can solve problems through helping each other and through collaboration.

It was an assembly I had practised in my substantive school Invicta Primary School in Blackheath, where I was the deputy headteacher. I felt confident that it would work well. However, I had not planned for the unexpected! With an audience of eight governors and 250 children, instead of learning the lessons of geese, one of the chosen pupils, Charlie (who also happened to be a governor's son), decided that, rather than feed fruit to his fellow pupil using his extra-long spoon, it would be more fun to improvise, using his spoon to scatter strawberries and mango slices into the air and catch them in his mouth. This not only caused havoc amongst the 250 pupils, who decided that they too should benefit from the showering of treats, but it also completely spoiled the message of the story – namely, collaboration helps us all achieve more. With nothing to lose, he then decided to fall backwards, knocking over the expensive sound system and inadvertently breaking my best assembly music CD!

Remarkably, I still got the job as headteacher. The learning?

1   It isn't your success that defines you but rather the responses to your failures and struggles. Learning is not a linear sequence of triumphs but a jumble of useful learning mistakes, which collectively help you grow 'skin in the game'.

2   Rather than avoiding making errors, we should embrace them as new possibilities – as long as we learn from them. An error-free world would not have given us medical discoveries, scientific breakthroughs or even new insight into how to lead school assemblies.

3   Context matters.

A new challenge

It was July 2013 when I was asked to consider taking on Woodhill Primary School, situated in the Royal Borough of Greenwich, a stubbornly 'requiring improvement' school saturated with support, initiatives and resources to help it improve. Reading schemes, behaviour reward systems, consultant leaders, local authority interventions and much more had been transplanted into the school, stitched together by a hotchpotch of policies, recommendations and non-negotiables. Just about everything had been tried to raise expectations and improve outcomes for the pupils, who came predominantly from the dilapidated social housing surrounding the school.

By December 2013, Woodhill was already improving, mainly thanks to my ten years' leadership experience at Bannockburn Primary School, where multiple mistakes guided me steadily towards an understanding of how schools *really* improve. Thank you, Charlie! During my time at Bannockburn, I learnt to avoid the following:

- Any policy or initiative that was delivered to the school in the form of a plastic laminated lunchbox containing DVDs preaching 'this is how you improve a school'.

- Schemes of work written by graduates who had never stepped foot inside a classroom, let alone had to teach Year 1 pupils during the autumn term.

- Self-proclaimed 'expert' teachers who were, typically, closed to learning, avoided risk-taking and believed their way was the only way.

- Behaviour improvement gimmicks that relied on elaborate incentives or external rewards, including golden time, dressing-up days, trips to the cinema or anything to do with popcorn.

- Teachers who believed you shouldn't smile for the first half term of any school year in case the children actually started to like you.

- Appointing staff who sent their own children to selective schools but thought that working with children from council estates was missionary work.

In other words, making lots of mistakes made me a better leader of learning and helped me improve Woodhill Primary School more quickly than I could have done otherwise. My learning from Bannockburn Primary School, where governors, staff and the community afforded me countless opportunities to mess things up, was critical to the success that Woodhill Primary School, and its sister school Foxfield Primary School, would later benefit from.

This is what is known as a 'black swan'. From the outside, my leadership of Bannockburn Primary School was viewed as dynamic, positive and impactful. The school became a National College support school, judged outstanding by Ofsted in all categories, and was generally regarded as one of the highest-performing schools. From the inside, the school was consistently fragile, bound by the quality of interactions between people, governed more deeply through relationships than by checklists or standards frameworks. It may have been the leaders who received the most praise, but the true story of Bannockburn's success was as much to do with the quality of premises and office staff, who created a climate for excellence to flourish, as any 'strategy'.

So, I arrived at Woodhill Primary School in September 2013 to a school in chaos, but with huge optimism that we could improve the school rapidly. Ofsted arrived just two months later and judged leadership to be 'good'. This was a turning point. Leadership had not been judged to be good at Woodhill for a generation. In April 2014, I was asked to become the executive headteacher at Foxfield Primary School, another Greenwich school, situated two miles east of Woodhill. It was a school waiting to be placed into special measures – quite literally.

The purpose of this book

This book explores how collaboration in the classroom and between schools can maximise our collective capital for learning. It is an element of our work that is neither celebrated enough nor used systemically across the school system as a lever for change. The prevailing narrative in education is one of uncompromising, focused leadership, high standards and accountability. However, according to Pasi Sahlberg, the highest-performing education systems globally invest much more in collaborative approaches to school improvement, which involve teachers working together to improve the whole system. School improvement, underpinned by mutual accountability at all levels, means that we take increasing responsibility for each other's learning as well as our own.

The opening chapters will examine the impact of high-stakes accountability in determining the mindset in education for sustainable improvement. This includes the role that school inspection has played in reducing autonomy and trust. In subsequent chapters, I will focus on the substance of learning and how, through the provision of an expansive education, we can ensure that all children receive the very best provision and all pupils can achieve the very best.

Throughout, I will attempt to make tangible the potential of a more meaningful way to improve school performance, where working deeply together in partnership with teachers, pupils and other schools binds learning experiences to values, helping young people and teachers make sense of the complex world we live in. In this book, I will tell you the story of two schools: Woodhill Primary School and Foxfield Primary School. As you read, I want you to think about these questions:

- Why is it that these two schools are achieving against the odds?
- Why are the staff so deeply committed to serving our children and communities?
- How do they create enduring relationships of mutual trust and respect?

The stories contained within belong to those who feel the injustice of an education system in which the narrative conflicts with the reality. It is for those who feel the pain caused by our addiction to policy reform, which has typically been based on fresh air and not much else, other than the whims of our politicians. Let this book provide encouragement and belief to all those who feel connected to a cause where teaching pupils how to learn to live is as important as teaching them what to learn.

A few words about collaboration

Before we get started, it is important to define what we mean by collaboration. I will argue multiple times that teachers' sense of collective agency is strongest when we take shared responsibility for each other's success and work together as change agents. There is solid evidence that 'collective efficacy' (the group willingness to translate thoughts and feelings into meaningful actions in order to make a difference) has a positive impact on pupil achievement (Eells, 2011; ATL, 2015). It also binds us together through a collective sense of purpose, which brings people closer as a community. It builds networks for improvement. This is what I mean by collaboration. It is a powerful tool when harnessed well, but there are some caveats.

Firstly, deep collaboration between teachers and schools necessitates thinking differently about the role of leadership, providing space for teams to engage with each other without the fear of judgement. Collaboration thrives best in a climate of trust and autonomy. This means that leadership has to be adept enough to operate multi-dimensionally. The leader (or leaders) must also be learners. Linked to this point, meaningful collaboration also necessitates a deep awareness of what Daniel Goleman calls 'triple focus'. For leaders to be effective in an age where the power of networks can determine success in a far more powerful way than an individual can, they need to operate with three key qualities:

> *'**Inner focus** attunes us to our intuitions [and] guiding values. **Other focus** smooths our connections to the people in our lives. And **outer focus** lets us navigate in the larger world. A leader tuned out of his internal world will be rudderless; one blind to the world of others will be clueless; those indifferent to the larger systems within which they operate will be blindsided.' (Goleman, 2013, p.11)*

Schools that foster a spirit of triple focus are most likely to generate collective agency, because their awareness of impact extends beyond their immediate setting. The role of school leader has most impact when they are continuously paying attention to the climate for collaboration in order for it to flourish in multiple ways. (See Table 1, p.5.)

Secondly, dictating that teachers should collaborate, without being strategic about how the collaboration will be facilitated creates false hope and unrealistic expectations. If we are true to our word about the importance of collaboration, time must be invested for it to work, and space must be provided for teachers to work together in new ways. In other words, forcing teachers to plan together does not mean that teachers will collaborate well. I have tried to illustrate the layers of collaboration with reference to professional development in Table 2 (p. 5) and will refer back to these points in subsequent chapters.

Table 1 The leadership of learning can be redefined within and between schools and across the system

Leading learning	How
Within schools	• Participate as a learner • Offer to share expertise • Engage in 'lesson study' research of learning • Develop bespoke CPD which engages in evidence-based approaches to improving teaching • Use collaborative groups to study, share and then monitor impact of learning • Blog, write up, evaluate and share impact of learning.
Between schools	• Empower and employ leaders to share expertise and experience between schools • Establish networks linked to subject development or enrichment of pedagogy • Build mentoring networks, hubs of excellence and 'teach meets' to review, reflect and evaluate impact of learning • Ensure priorities reflect improvement needs • Champion excellence, build trust and release talent.
Across the system	• Share knowledge and learning openly • Give away ideas • Write up and publish learning from research • Engage in research networks • Refine excellence through continuous revision and review.

Table 2 Professional development can be redefined through layers of collaboration

Leading CPD	How
Improving knowledge and skills	• Focused cross-partnership learning walks and excellence visits programmes • Production of policies and toolkits • Development of shared thinking through seminars and masterclasses • Networking events • Focused school reviews (linked to an identified area of development).
What we do	• Lesson study • Action research • Peer coaching and mentoring • Lead practitioners moving between schools to support teaching and learning • Shared induction programmes • Sharing practice through blogging, production of shared resources.
Gaining impact	• New knowledge gained and systems refined (policies, practice and resources) • Teachers feel better connected across partnerships • Excellence developed in specific areas (leads to innovation) • Organisation is 'learner orientated' across groups within school • Pupil experiences enhanced across learning disciplines.

Let's start this story by exploring the role that accountability plays in education and its impact on our teacher mindset for improvement. While our logical, 'system two' thinking (Kahneman, 2011) calls for discipline, structure and sequential planned improvement, lasting change takes place when we unleash the counter-intuitive 'system one' possibilities, giving greater value to discretionary effort and recognising the non-linear nature of change.

This book is accompanied by online resources including:

- Tables from the book
- The Woodhill Primary School transformation plan
- The Foxfield Primary School transformation plan.

Visit www.bloomsbury.com/manifesto-for-excellence for more information.

1 Let's start with why

It is here that the story begins, but first we need to briefly examine the pitfalls of hubris in school leadership and how accountability in education has misplaced trust in policy to deliver change, rather than in people. We will explore how imposed accountability undermines confidence, erodes trust and distorts the reality of authentic school improvement.

If our education system is reflective of the world in which we live, it is fair to say that we are in crisis. The word 'crisis' derives from ancient Greek and translates into 'separate' or 'sieve'. In other words, a crisis should offer a moment of truth and reflection. Our failure to close achievement gaps, continued low levels of equity between schools nationally and increased test-based competition amongst pupils represents a collective policy failure. According to the Varkey Foundation's Generation Z survey (2017), we have, amongst our pupils, some of the unhappiest young people, with the lowest levels of emotional wellbeing. Our faith in politicians to help us find solutions has evaporated; teacher and leadership recruitment in schools are at chronic levels. This is indeed a crisis.

The question is this: what are we going to do about it?

To begin, we have to challenge the notion that more accountability per se is what makes the difference. By this I include excessive testing, hierarchy, top-down leadership and an obsession with formal monitoring. This isn't how the best school systems improve, as demonstrated in Table 3, p. 8. In fact, the correlation between accountability frameworks and school impact is, at best, ambiguous. I include in this catch-all of accountability: Ofsted, Mocksted, assessment reform, (some) governance structures and various compliance-check models. After 25 years of test-based improvement culture, we still have wide discrepancies between high- and low-performing schools and large achievement gaps between pupil groups. If accountability was the answer, we would have reduced this discrepancy by now. The school improvement narrative is still one that emphasises 'proving' rather than 'improving' outcomes for pupils – it has become so institutionalised that schools lead through fear, risk-aversion and compliance. Despite the myth-busting, our education behaviours concentrate on test-based rather than trust-based approaches to improving the whole system.

Education policy has bounced from one initiative to another, epitomised by the frequency in change of ministerial leadership and chasing the latest education fad to fix another problem. There has been little strategy in designing a vision for how our schools might become beacons of hope in a time when social inequality, our sense of community and increasing geo-political uncertainty darken our world.

At the same time, the concept of teaching and education as a craft or an art has been replaced by instruction. The impact leads us to believe that learning happens in straightforward, rather than messy, uncertain jumps. It supports a view that change happens in a predictably straight line, making it easier to track, or by pulling levers (more phonics, more discipline, more testing, more mastery teaching). In other words, there is an ordered, logical, sequential approach to school improvement – a delivery model instead of a design model.

Table 3 The differences between self-inspection and self-evaluation system models are clear

Self-inspection	Self-evaluation
Top-down	Bottom-up
A one-off event	Continuous
Provides a snapshot	Offers an evolving picture
Time-consuming	Time-saving
Accountability-focused	Improvement-focused
Based on a rigid framework	Flexible and spontaneous
Uses existing predetermined criteria	Creates relevant criteria
Can detract from teaching and learning	Improves teaching and learning
Avoids risks	Takes risks

We have encouraged schools to play safe, follow the rules, take fewer risks. The trade-offs are quick wins, measured by headline-grabbing policies against the long-term investment in professional judgement and an educational values base crafted to meet the needs of twenty-first-century learners. We have reduced the life-changing work that teachers do to a binary metric. This effectively simplifies teaching to tasks or outputs instead of recognising the complexity of learning as an exchange, an interaction, a combustion of multiple experiences, splattered with 'useful learning mistakes'. School improvement that places creation and shared ownership at the centre imbues a collective sense of worth. Stuff that is done for quick wins, functions or efficiency wears us down.

A crisis in teaching

The Association for Teachers and Lecturers union surveyed newly qualified teachers (NQTs) in 2015, asking what their motives were for becoming teachers. Of the 858 respondents, over 80 per cent responded that they enjoyed working with young people and 75 per cent said that they wanted to make a difference. Nearly 80 per cent of respondents described the excitement of celebrating pupils' 'lightbulb moments' as a significant reason to enjoy teaching. Almost half of participants spoke about the benefits of collaboration with other teachers and 70 per cent referenced time to reflect on their practice as something they would welcome more of. Teachers, it seems, place greater emphasis on the 'why' of teaching than the more pragmatic 'what' and 'hows'. Agency, moral purpose and a sense of commitment to pupils are powerful tools – especially in adversity.

Of those teachers who took part in the 2015 survey, a frightening proportion will have left the profession already. Government figures for dropout rates for teachers in their first five years of work are over 30 per cent. Their main reasons will have been the pressures caused by teacher workload, the negative public perception of teachers portrayed in the media and concerns about pupils' behaviour in our schools. If teachers most value the connection between their work and its immediate impact on learning, they also recognise that much of what we do has no direct impact on raising standards or improving life chances. The continued emphasis on accountability, typified by being busy, is still viewed by teachers as the main reason for them leaving the profession.

The problem of accountability

The education system in the UK is buckling under the pressure of intense accountability. The current state of affairs may have started life as a crack in the ice, through which the autonomy of schools fell in the 1990s, but it is now triggering unrest and disillusionment as we wake up to the reality that the system isn't working. We have allowed accountability to become the defining narrative of our schools – one where success is measured as a test score or an inspection. This is what Daniel Kahneman, the Nobel Prize-winning psychologist, describes as a 'cognitive illusion'. Put simply, it means that the performance metrics we have used for the past 25 years have failed and threaten to do so again. To date, there has been a vacuum of education and economic policy capable of setting out concrete actions to heal the fracture.

Between 2007 and 2017, we have had four Secretaries of State for Education, including Michael Gove, who served the longest term of office between 2010 and 2014. In this same period, we have seen the publication of well over 100 Education Acts, Reports and White Papers, including:

- 2007: The Children's Plan
- 2009: Rose Review of Primary Education
- 2009: White Paper: Your Child, Your Schools, Our Future
- 2010: Cambridge Primary Review
- 2010: Children, Schools and Families Act
- 2011: Academies Act
- 2013: New National Curriculum
- 2016: Education and Adoption Act.

The trouble with being accountable to so many different masters is that they all have their own vision for what education should look like. Consistently inconsistent policymaking of this kind has resulted in us failing to meet the challenge of delivering a transformational education for *all* children – one that closes attainment gaps, increases equity, delivers social justice and provides a deeper sense of commitment to global citizenship.

Too few disadvantaged pupils go on to gain entry into our best universities, the gap in attainment between the most affluent and poorest pupils still exists and our lowest-performing schools are still most likely to be situated amongst the lowest socio-economic communities. Our system-wide inability to narrow achievement gaps between our most and least privileged pupils stands out sharply against claims from Ofsted that our schools are better now than ever before. It challenges the assumption that our accountability mechanisms are working for all pupils.

Throughout this book I will challenge the assumptions and myths about education that we have historically accepted, about how accountability can build a secure system founded on equity, social justice and a belief in the entitlement for all pupils to be provided with the best education experiences. I will offer an alternative vision for learning that equips pupils with the skills and learning dispositions to thrive in an increasingly complex and socially diverse world.

The Ofsted model for accountability

The Office for Standards in Education has evolved to become an infallible, untouchable institution within the English education system. It has played a significant role in determining what we value, shaping cultural beliefs about how schools operate and work with each other to improve outcomes for pupils. This has perpetuated beliefs and behaviours that impact daily on the work of teachers to the point where we think in leadership *actions* not *interactions*. Formal book looks, whole-school progress review meetings and monitoring become artificial, stage-managed improvement tasks, delivered so that we *play* the role of leadership. There is a perception gap between the true impact of formal monitoring and its intended impact. In other words, just because you have monitored books, it doesn't mean that it has made a blind bit of difference.

It doesn't have to be like this though. Giving permission for teachers to lead their own self-evaluation, making school improvement a collaborative process, has the double advantage of:

- growing skin in the game (e.g. helping teachers learn from experience)
- creating agency amongst staff to find solutions to common school challenges.

Schools obsess about data reporting for external accountability instead of focusing on how quality formative assessment can be used to maximise learning. Setting national or local education targets based purely on attainment in a limited number of subjects defies everything we know about expansive assessment practice. It creates a fixed mindset about what constitutes success and ignores the broader skills family that employers are desperate for our young people to demonstrate.

Fundamentally, the inspection system misses the point that lasting success is built by learning from error; innovation and excellence is fuelled by multiple failures, and learning from our own mistakes is compulsory. But the fear and paralysis felt by teachers and leaders at the mere thought of 'getting the call' is indicative of the 'proving culture' that the inspection system has created. Leaders know only too well how much an inspection result can alter pathways for schools and their staff, and how this industrial approach to evaluating schools is completely at odds with how our most successful schools thrive (see Table 4).

Table 4 Schools operating within a 'proving culture' suffer paralysis rather than growth

	School-improving culture	Proving culture
Key drivers for behaviour and action	To increase learning and build autonomous, distributed leadership	To judge and evaluation through quality control
Focused on	Building teaching quality and improving practice across system	Measuring performance and pupil achievement through instruction
Dominant hierarchy	Bottom up	Top down
Dominant processes	Informative and responsive	Reactive
Dominant methodology	Learn from mistakes: use all available evidence to inform decision making and set priorities within the local and national context	Follow rules: priorities are pre-determined by the Ofsted handbook
Dominant climate	We value learning mistakes as new opportunities to grow stronger together	We fear mistakes and error making as indicative of failure
Dominant response	We want to share learning and growth. We want to maximise learning opportunities collectively for the good of all children	We believe in hierarch. We keep our successes to ourselves and hide any flaws in what we do. Don't question our authority!
Impact	Growth: creativity flourishes; innovation and risk taking ensures incremental gains maximise learning of whole organisation. The power of learning is collective and turbo charged. This, in turn, 'grows' new ideas and new leaders.	Paralysis: fear of failure sets the tone; hierarchical deference to Ofsted inhibits teamwork; opportunities for new learning are missed because conformity to instruction dominates. This in turn inhibits potential leaders from taking risks or sharing learning not considered 'worthy' enough.

The logic of standards-based education is deceptively simple: schools use accountability to measure what works best and evaluate the outcomes by benchmarking standards against predictions and the performance standards of similar schools. Local authorities, MATs (multi-academy trusts) and Ofsted provide additional layers of accountability by testing a school's ability to evaluate its performance accurately using a nationally-agreed framework. The evidence from inspection and self-review is used to self-justify intervention, leadership actions and, inevitably, more accountability measures. When we view the world through this lens, we behave accordingly. We believe that it is our tracking of outcomes that makes the difference, rather than the interactions between staff and pupils. We invent a narrative that inflates the impact of leadership tasks, ignoring the 'incidental moments' between teacher and pupil that are the real, but often hidden, cause of an improvement.

This has seen schools compete against each other rather than collaborate; it has engendered a climate of fear, where teachers hide mistakes, take fewer risks and squirrel away their best ideas. When Ofsted first inspected Foxfield Primary School in 2014, it was clear that the fear of inspection was a major barrier to risk-taking. Teachers lamented that 'We can't possibly do that' or 'We won't be allowed to…'. The shadow of accountability dictated the tempo and narrative of change across the school. It created fear and reduced confidence in taking risks. The most perverse manifestation of this paralysis is our limp acceptance of assessment reforms that have reduced children to labels of 'pass' or 'fail'. When Key Stage 2 test scores are made public in July, our 11-year-olds will be judged not by their potential or worth as citizens – their capacity to make a bigger difference – but instead by whether they have met 'expected' standards or not. It is a binary model – the metrics for success are set to pass or fail, a gloomy world view that values only the performance rather than the journey of learning.

This can change quickly though. It was refreshing to hear the Chief Inspector-Designate Amanda Spielman, speaking in 2016 at the Education Committee, saying that it was 'highly likely we will end up with a multi-layered inspections model' (Wiggins, 2016). She described this as a 'good development'. Hopefully, this will lead to an inspection framework that is rigorous but reflects the plurality of our education system. How different might our schools be if we used broader metrics to evaluate the successes of learning, including our willingness to take risks, learn from error and the benefits of learning from others?

Assessment as accountability

Our shallow interpretation of assessment has confused summative (test-based) with formative (diagnostic) assessment to the point where we view learning as levels instead of skills. This has impacted on how we view pupils as individuals. We have learnt to see children, with all the unique gifts they bring, as numbers. A child not learning at the right number becomes an inconvenience or, worse still, an excuse to fail. This has left a legacy whereby teacher performance, including performance management, has become reliant on the need to deliver targets for achievement based on the performance of children in test conditions – as though this was ever the best way to evaluate and quantify the work we do in complex classrooms, where relationships, collaboration and learning dispositions matter most. Pupil numbers, in terms of test outcomes, have provided leverage for governors to base decisions about salary increases. This has led to schools gaming the system and inflating pupils' actual scores, so fearful and paranoid have we become about accountability.

The effect this has had on school leadership is also damaging. Just as teacher autonomy has eroded, so too has leadership confidence. Many of us have made decisions about professional development because of pre-populated national strategy 'Raising Attainment Plan' templates. Leadership has been mechanical and instructional rather than dynamic, responsive and rooted in community needs. Many school leaders have lacked the confidence to balance political objectives with school-based evidence (in knowing what was right for children), alongside the in-school capacity to deliver. Many schools have developed school policy because of external factors, instead of having the confidence to wave away the series of latest fads or interventions.

Another way

Mature school improvement is founded on high levels of trust and shared accountability for each other's learning. It places greater emphasis on embedding leadership learning, instead of continuously seeking to measure outcomes. Professional capital and investment in people leads to mutual accountability. Just ask participants from the Greater London Authority's Getting Ahead London coaching programme what they have valued most and they will tell you that it's all about the collaboration, sharing ideas and learning together – the network! Networks flip the theory that growth and development reside solely in headteachers' offices, instead placing much greater emphasis on co-construction and social capital. Fundamentally, learning is a social activity and has the greatest potential to flourish when it is developed with others' participation, engagement and common ownership of problems.

In an era of networks, it is the power of the group to make a collective difference that becomes more significant than a school's ability to meet a compliance checklist. While the latter ensures improvement through targets and performance indicators (largely reliant on pupil achievement, which varies), the former provides a model for organic learning and organisational growth, which is driven by practitioners defining what matters most within their context. It is the former that provides a maturity model for sustainable school improvement that is bottom-up, rather than top-down.

Leadership and accountability

Comparisons between leadership within schools and the medical profession highlight the complexity of leadership in organisations where relationships within a community define success or failure. Process management systems should not replace professional judgement and are often overly focused on deficiencies rather than assets, such as people.

By contrast, the investment in relationships across a community enhances the social capital of the whole, rather than the individual, and also creates a cause for improvement. It is this discretionary effort that underpins the fabric of a learning community and dictates the pace and tone of improvement.

Discretionary effort

Another myth of leadership is that it is born from individual courage, strength, determination and certainty. Unchecked, this creates hubris and leads to blind spots and trap doors, which can be difficult to climb out of. We read the stories of unwavering heroes standing firm, reaching out in perilous storms as waves crash against the rocks. The true narrative of leadership, however, is one of collaboration, relationships and also counter-intuition. It is not the individual leaders who make for success but rather collective leadership, which establishes a critical mass for actions to build momentum – building 'discretionary effort' amongst teams. The tipping point for schools that create enduring leadership is that they lean more towards an enabling model, where staff of all levels feel empowered to innovate, create and 'grow' school improvement. At Foxfield Primary School, when the school was placed in special measures, it wasn't individuals who rewrote the script, helping the school turn around in record time; it was the collective efforts of staff across both Woodhill and Foxfield, who gave a shared commitment to helping each other improve. Their actions changed behaviours and forged new beliefs about what schools should do more or less of when faced with adversity. Unsurprisingly, 'more of' consisted of collaboration.

Building community is always associated with leadership, is harder to evaluate and is not necessarily included in any accountability framework. However, it is the community that generates social and moral capital, leading to lasting improvement. Discretionary effort is aligned with a values-based approach to school improvement, which ensures that:

1 Learning communities are developed by focusing on peoples' gifts rather than deficiencies.

2 Accountability is co-created through engagement with change as a collaborative process.

3 Group success is driven by relationships.

4 Lasting improvements take place because teams are empowered to act.

5 Possibilities for change are strengthened when they are declared publicly.

6 Success is achieved through harnessing the social capital of the whole group.

While leaders may want to fall back on what they know, measure leadership through actions, set higher expectations and do everything themselves, the leadership fallacy often derails success, creates the wrong climate and demotivates people instead of inspiring them. Leadership blind spots, often the result of past successes, where leaders replicate a formula for past achievements, are crude tools if left unchecked. Good ideas travel well, but with nuance. My 'long spoons' assembly, delivered successfully at one school, was not preordained to be successful in the next – this is why generic plans often fail. Put simply, there is no such thing as guaranteed success, even if you have had success in the past.

For this reason, the best leadership encourages challenge, welcomes difference and embraces the 'useful learning mistakes' as exciting new possibilities. As the saying goes, your grandmother's hard-earned wisdom is often worth more than overinflated theory. Hard-earned wisdom can only be put to use in an environment where mistake-making and learning-centred leadership is encouraged.

Key questions to consider:

1 How does your school harness collaboration to best effect in order to lead change and how do you know its impact?
2 How does your school create the climate and conditions for teams to flourish?
3 Do leaders spend more of their time interacting with others or instructing others?
4 How does your school use error-making as an opportunity to relearn or reflect?
5 In what ways are mistakes valued or celebrated?
6 How does your school notice and value discretionary effort amongst teams?

A vicious consequence of top-down (contrasted with mutual) accountability is that it creates hierarchy-dependent expertise: the inspector, the politician, the policymaker. In the next chapter, we will consider what happened at Foxfield Primary School when Ofsted visited. This will allow us to answer the following questions: Who are the real experts? Who determines who the experts should be? We will also reflect on what happens when the inspectors have left the building.

2 When Ofsted came to call

Ten years of headship experience at Bannockburn Primary School, working with open-to-learning, 'bottom-up' rather than 'top-down' believers in school improvement, gave me 'skin in the game'. Expertise in understanding learning and school leadership was co-constructed amongst peers over time. We saw ourselves as 'designers of learning'. Designers of learning demonstrate commitment to mastery as a journey instead of a finished piece. Viewed this way, the practice becomes as, or more, important than the performance.

I have already argued that consultants, policymakers, politicians and inspectors measure school effectiveness through instruction rather than design. These are people better able to advise on one-dimensional solutions than to understand the complexity of leading through relationships. They think in single steps, actions and obvious solutions; they value the outcome of the performance as greater than the journey or the struggle.

In this chapter, we explore the importance of risk-taking and shared responsibility for redefining what matters in education, so that we are not reliant on those who have never delivered, never taught or failed and picked themselves up again, to determine the future. We will also challenge the myth that school partnerships work best when one school is perceived to be the stronger (donor school) supporting the weaker (receiver school).

In April 2014, I became executive headteacher at Foxfield Primary School in South East London, after having been in post as head at Woodhill Primary School, its partner school, for just six months. At the time, Woodhill Primary School was still judged to be requiring improvement (but with good leadership) and Foxfield Primary School was about to be placed in special measures. This unusual partnership was established by a forward-thinking local authority, which understood that partnerships work in all contexts and that through collaboration both schools could improve rapidly. Geographically, the schools were close and both schools served communities of a similar demographic.

Two weeks after taking over as the new executive headteacher at Foxfield, Ofsted came to call.

Desperate times…

I remember feeling confident and bullish on the first day of the Foxfield inspection. My experience of inspection at Woodhill was largely a positive one. The inspection team understood the journey the school was on and gave credit for the changes we had already begun to make. The team was challenging but listened. They posed tough questions but wanted to work with us. I was feeling so confident for Foxfield, given my previous experience, that I decided to don my favourite cream linen summer suit by way of demonstrating to staff, children and the inspection team that the two days to come were going to be full of sunshine and good news! That was perhaps mistake number one; by mid-morning, my linen jacket, creased and sweat-stained, was slung across the office desk as I manically raced around the building in search of good teaching.

By lunchtime of day one, it was clear that the inspection team were forming unfavourable judgements about the school. We were told that they had looked up the name of the school online and found video footage of pupils on school premises at the weekend, drinking alcohol and smoking. Governors from the school informed the inspection team that the school had built large reserves of funding, which should have been invested in the children. Older pupils described how the curriculum had been narrowed to the point that learning consisted mainly of test practice for reading, writing and maths. The lead inspector, full of agitation, informed me that she had heard a pupil tell another pupil to 'shut up' in the middle of a lesson, and a joint observation in a Reception class led to the inspector citing chapter-and-verse health and safety concerns:

> *'Pupils, especially boys, have difficulty managing their own behaviour. In lessons where activities fail to enthuse them to want to learn, they lose concentration and distract others from learning. Young children squabble, finding it hard to share resources or take turns. In the playground behaviour is overly boisterous. Some pupils miss their playtimes because they have been involved in fighting.' (Ofsted, 2014)*

Under pressure from the local authority to help secure the best possible judgement for the school, we did all we could to tell a narrative of change. We shared action plans, showed them examples of pupil books that had been 'fresh started' and drew extensively on our experiences in leading schools of similar context to a better place – including Woodhill Primary School, where leadership had been described as 'inspirational' just four months earlier. But the reality was, having only been in post for two weeks, our impact had been minimal. Although we started afresh with new books for all pupils – to give children the message that our expectations from hereon in were going to be higher – there was little evidence of learning for these newly tacky-backed books to be taken seriously. During the mid-afternoon day one 'book look', the evidence was stark. Scribbled answers, disjointed learning sequences, little pride taken in the joy of learning – it was evident across the curriculum. Learning was not marked, and much of what children produced in their books was of such a low standard that the inspection team suggested pupils were working years below their age-related standards. The final report commented that:

> *'Pupils' books show that typically, progress is slow across the school. They often work at levels lower than those expected for their age. This is because expectations of what they can do are too low.' (Ofsted, 2014)*

…desperate measures

But still we fought on. The one glimmer of hope we had was that the best teaching in the school was in Year 6. Inspectors had missed out on observing these classes because the inspection coincided with the national Key Stage 2 tests, so children were either sitting tests or preparing for them. On day two, however, there were no tests. The Head of School Improvement for Greenwich was meeting the lead inspector on the morning of day two, before school, so we thought this would be a good opportunity to demonstrate what children could do at the top end of the school. The teachers were prepared and actually looking forward to showcasing some strong teaching.

The plan was for the School Improvement Head to meet with the senior HMI inspector until around 9.15 am, before I would then encourage her to accompany me in joint observations of our oldest pupils' lessons. We would try our best to place in context the rapid successes at Woodhill School and the journey that Foxfield had just begun. We both believed that this would encourage the inspection team to recognise leadership capacity in the school.

However, by 9.30 am, my amygdala was twitching. Thoughts raced through my mind: 'The meeting seems very long. What's going on? It must be worse than I thought? The HMI *needs* to see Year 6! I know, I'll interrupt the meeting and *make* her observe with me.' Without a pause, I burst into the meeting room, stopped the conversation in its tracks and let the words drop from my mouth: 'There's teaching happening in Year 6 and you are in here! You are about to place this school into a category and haven't even seen our oldest pupils learning. You need to see Year 6 – immediately!'

It was not the wisest move. Calmly, the lead inspector finished her sentence and methodically gathered up her things. Realising the misjudgement of both tone and words, I stood sheepishly, waiting for her to follow me out. Instead, she ignored me and walked straight past me into the main corridor.

Things continued to get worse

Year 6 classrooms were at the end of the corridor, on the right-hand side and up a flight of stairs. I watched from the reception area as the lead inspector walked along the corridor and, instead of turning right for the staircase, embarked left and headed straight into a Year 4 classroom. What was going on? Had she made a mistake? She had spent nearly a day and a half in the school, had pretty much condemned it to special measures but had not even seen any teaching in one of the most crucial year groups in any school. This was not good, and the situation was made worse by the fact that the classroom she had walked into belonged to a teacher whom we already had serious concerns about. I decided to take matters into my own hands again. If nothing else, we wouldn't go down without a fight. Walking stealthily past the classroom, I glanced in to scan the layout and plan my manoeuvre. Thankfully, the inspector was sat at the back of the room, flicking through pupils' books. This was good. If I could sneak in on the right, below the display table, she might not see me. This would mean that I might be able to help the lesson by coaching the teacher. It seemed like the right thing to do.

With the door slightly open, getting into the lesson was easier than I had expected. The lead inspector was intently browsing through books and making notes. She hadn't seen me – but neither had the teacher. I crept in low and sat on the floor below table level, adjacent to a group of pupils near to the door. In my ecstasy at being able to get into the class without being spotted, I allowed my mind to wander. 'We should do this more often,' I thought. 'We could rig up coaching headphones, with cameras, to support teachers in "real time"'.

The reality of poor teaching in the classroom shook me back into the room. The lesson was not good. The teacher was nervous and didn't introduce the key teaching points well. Fluffing her way through, children were confused about the learning content. A few began to disengage and talk over her. However, being nervous, she hadn't seen what was happening. I had to do something. If I could somehow intervene, without being seen or heard, we could still pull this off. But what to suggest? I know – a mini plenary! The teacher hadn't connected that pupils were disengaging because they didn't understand the core teaching concepts. She was now starting to lose patience – reverting to telling pupils off and pausing for every child to give their full attention. All it did was prolong the agony, compound the misunderstandings and increase off-task behaviour.

'Mini-plenary,' I whispered in a soft voice from below the table. She didn't hear me. 'Introduce a mini-plenary,' I whispered again, slightly louder. Still no response. 'Mini plenary!', falling just short of yelling it at her. That got her attention! However, instead of a poised recall for the whole class to recap on their prior learning, utilising the strength of collaboration between pupils, the teacher responded with a very public and slightly aggressive, 'What!? Who said that?' This was followed by an even more pronounced stagger-cum-sway as she turned around to see where the mystery voice originated from.

At this point, I was thinking that the situation was still salvageable. At the very least, if the lead inspector saw me in the classroom, on the floor whispering advice, she would have to respect my knowledge of teaching and learning and the fact that I was skilled enough to diagnose what the lesson was absolutely crying out for. The class teacher, though, had other intentions. As she swung round, determined to know who was disrupting her lesson, she crashed into the whiteboard easel, causing it to topple over. Thirty pupils gave an audible gasp as the easel narrowly missed landing on a group of children sat to the teacher's left-hand side. To make matters worse, the class teacher, clutching her thigh, stopped the lesson completely, shouting, 'My leg, my leg! I can't feel my leg!' Not content with this, she then proceeded to drag her newly injured leg around the room with her as though it were an unwelcome appendage strapped onto her body. I sat there helpless on the floor, while the lead inspector strode across the classroom, nodded politely in my direction, then walked out of the room.

It was at this point that even I had to admit that the writing was on the wall. I stood up, checked that the teacher didn't require first aid, and left the room.

Identity crisis

Grizzled and frowning intently, I sat through the inspection feedback meeting, shoulders hunched, arms wrapped around tightly, emotions floating between anger, frustration and outright fear. Clutching at every word, I was desperate for a phrase or sentence that might provide just enough comfort to convince me that things would be okay. All I needed was some small affirmation or sign that the new leadership team (which of course included me) were the right people to turn this school around. In that meeting, my identity as an experienced headteacher was reduced to scratching through unforgiving sentences for a crumb of belief in my qualities to successfully lead this school.

Alongside me, the local authority lead for primary schools glared defiantly at the lead inspector, assessing the full impact of every word, before offering kinder eyes to me and the (still-to-be-appointed) new headteacher of the school, Rupinder Bansil. Sitting next to Rupinder, the outgoing chair of governors stoically accepted her fate as we heard the grim litigation – a scathing list of charges in failing to provide appropriate education for a school serving more than 700 pupils in one of London's most underprivileged communities. Amongst the accusations:

1 Leaders, managers and governors have not taken the action needed to stop the decline in achievement, behaviour and the quality of teaching since the previous inspection. Their view of the school's effectiveness is not accurate.

2 In Year 2 pupils' attainment in reading, writing and mathematics has remained low for several years. Pupils' progress from Years 3 to 6 is slow. Staff are not held accountable for what pupils achieve.

3 Too much teaching is inadequate. Staff are not sufficiently ambitious for pupils' achievements. Checks on what pupils know are not used to help teachers plan work that is at the right level of challenge for pupils. Teaching assistants are not used well enough to accelerate pupils' learning.

4 Feedback in lessons and marking do not help pupils to know how well they are doing or what they need to do to improve.

5 Children in the nursery and reception do not make a good start to their education. They are not prepared well for Year 1.

6 Pupils do not behave well in lessons, in the playground or at lunchtime. They lack respect for one another and the staff. Leaders have not yet established a culture that

prevents bullying or helps pupils to develop the skills to prevent it. They have not identified the underlying causes of disruptive behaviour.

7   Pupils do not enjoy a rich, broad and balanced programme of work. Subjects fail to engage their interest, especially boys. Pupils too often lose concentration, and take little pride in presenting their work neatly.

8   Governors have not secured strong and effective leadership over time. Not all governors and staff have the subject knowledge or training to carry out their roles well. Plans to improve the school rapidly are too new to have had an impact.

9   Leaders do not use information robustly to check that all pupil groups achieve equally well.

10 Parents do not have confidence in the school. Over half of those responding to the questionnaire would not recommend it to others. (Ofsted, 2014)

The verdict

In a calm, deflecting tone, the lead inspector systematically worked through the key issues, confirming that Foxfield Primary School was now in special measures. A brief intervention disrupted her flow but it was no more than a limp protest. Faltering only briefly, she drew on experience of having done this before – the Ofsted handbook was both her loyal servant and most dangerous weapon. No room for gallows humour or interruption here.

On 16 May 2014, Foxfield Primary School was judged to be an inadequate school in all areas of the inspection handbook. It seemed that our fate was sealed.

What came before?

My world was very different before 13 May 2014. It was my second full week in post as the new executive headteacher of Foxfield Primary School in South East London. Having successfully navigated an inspection at nearby Woodhill School, just four months earlier, the world seemed full of possibilities. The inspection at Woodhill happened nine weeks after my appointment, providing enough time to demonstrate at least some impact. Leadership was described as 'inspirational' and inspectors recognised that change was afoot. Only two years before that, I led a successful primary school partnership between Bannockburn and Rockliffe Manor Primary School, which was consistently in the top ten per cent of schools nationally; I was a National Leader in Education (NLE) and supported struggling schools across the country.

On accepting the challenge of Foxfield Primary School, I knew that the school faced significant difficulties but also believed we had the tools, conviction and desire to make the difference required. Before the inspection, we delivered a review of teaching to ascertain strengths and areas for development, and had given feedback to teachers about how we were going to shape the future. This led to tough conversations about school expectations for planning, curriculum design and core teaching non-negotiables, but people were up for the challenge. We knew that an inspection was pending and that it would likely have a negative outcome. We agreed that the school was not in a good place but felt, with enough time, we could demonstrate the same capacity we had brought to Woodhill Primary School, which – to be honest – educationally was in a worse place than Foxfield.

What we could not anticipate was the formality of the inspection. From the outset, the team gave no credit for my previous experience in school improvement, including the capacity we drew on from both Woodhill and Bannockburn primary schools. Nor did it matter that I had only been in post for two weeks and had chosen to join Foxfield knowing that it was a failing school. The tone of inspection was not in any way developmental or framed within a dialogue amongst professionals working for the same outcomes. It felt, quite honestly, like a betrayal of trust and faith in the much-lauded system leadership, which we believed would craft and influence better outcomes for children on a national scale.

Just one month earlier, Ofsted announced that school leaders working in failing schools *would* be given more time to demonstrate impact. This was celebrated by trade unions as a positive step. What happened to that? The *TES* reported that:

> 'In a letter to ASCL general secretary Brian Lightman, Sir Michael acknowledges that "headteachers of these schools need to be given sufficient time to address the various difficulties that face them". He also accepts that "Ofsted needs to play its part in encouraging our best and most ambitious leaders to go into our most challenging schools".' (Exley, 2014)

The announcement came against a backdrop of criticism from headteachers, fearful about the impact of heavy-handed inspection culture. *The Guardian* asked whether one disappointing Ofsted report could see the end of your career. The headline, 'A poor Ofsted report could lead to headteachers being "disappeared"' (Lepkowska, 2014), played to imagery of Lord Voldemort proportions. Headteachers spoke of 'leaked documents', which spelled out exactly how councils would deal with failing heads, including placing them on gardening leave or worse. Vic Goddard, the successful headteacher featured on the TV show *Educating Essex*, shared his concerns:

> 'No one could possibly believe sacking heads after two years in the job is a good idea. In areas where local authorities adopt this sort of draconian approach, you will have a ticking time bomb of headteacher shortages.' (Lepkowska, 2014)

After the verdict at Foxfield had been delivered, the inspection team vanished from the school, bags already packed in anticipation. Not one word of solace and certainly no reassurances or sympathy. We had already told staff to go home and so the school was empty, apart from Rupinder, the local authority lead and myself. As I emerged into the sunlight at around 5.30 pm on Friday 16 May, walking slowly away from the school entrance, a multitude of thoughts swirled inside my head: How would we tell parents? What would be the impact of the inspection on children? Where do we start in addressing the key issues? What about my career? Can I do this? Standing next to me was Rupinder. She hadn't even signed a contract or formally accepted the position to come and work at Foxfield. Yet here she was, grieving alongside me for the education of children she hadn't yet learnt the names of. What was she thinking, I wondered? Was this something she wanted or had the energy to take on? By joining Foxfield, she would be leaving behind an outstanding school where she was known and respected across the community, adored by the children and surrounded by excellent teachers who were capacity-givers. Leading the turnaround at Foxfield would be a big job, even more so now that we had official confirmation that we were an inadequate school – even more so with such a damning report. We required special measures. It doesn't get more serious than that.

What did the future hold?

As we approached the car park together, it felt like a lot had changed in two days. I felt diminished. It brought home the fragility of headship and the risks in choosing to work with vulnerable schools.

My identity as a school leader was bound almost entirely on the limitations of a national accountability framework that was without nuance or empathy. In being the executive headteacher of a failing school, I was no longer eligible to serve as a National Leader of Education and ceased to be part of the thriving local teaching school, for which I had helped write the successful bid. I was dropped from the list of attendees for regional policy meetings and pretty much told to stay at the school to sort things out. This was an unintended consequence of a one-dimensional model for school improvement, which has been the instrument of choice for the past 25 years in the English education system. I felt let down but guilty too. I placed my faith in a system meant to support and protect those committed school leaders who chose to work in our most challenged schools. I joined the school to clear up the mess but also felt responsible for creating it.

Both Rupinder and I agreed not to make any hasty decisions. We resolved to support each other through the coming days and then, before getting in our cars, we shed a mutual tear for the children and probably for ourselves too. It wasn't their fault. We both knew that. What we didn't yet know was that we were going to embark on the most amazing journey, which would flip the narrative of school improvement upside down and inside out. What happened next reframed the parameters of success for our children and our community. What started off as our story became the children's. It would be a journey of collaboration and partnership, which we hope has the potential to change the way we view school improvement in our country for ever.

Before I close this chapter, it is worth considering whether Ofsted did in fact make the right call by placing Foxfield Primary School into special measures. There are three very plausible arguments:

1   The inspection only served to confirm what we already knew and had plans to tackle. The published report should have acknowledged that the new leadership in place was fit for purpose to tackle these challenges.

2   Such a damning inspection outcome actually provided leverage to make the required changes. The failure of the school was a catalyst, which gave the new leadership team momentum.

3   The 'experience' of the inspection, including the exposure of the school's failings, perversely helped grow resilience amongst staff so that we could tackle the problems we faced.

In the next chapter, we will explore the concept of being both 'strategic' and 'deep seeking' leaders. Both approaches require exposure to failure and risk-taking so that we build authentic leadership. If the strategy concerns 'whats' and 'hows', the deep seeking connects to moral purpose and 'whys'.

3 Making plans

The final Ofsted report was published on the last day of the summer term 2014, confirming that Foxfield Primary School had been placed into special measures. It felt like an interminable length of time for our fate to be revealed – during which period an embargo prevented us from speaking about the inspection outcome with staff or the wider community. A small, hopeful part of me pretended that Ofsted had forgotten about the inspection, that the report would somehow be erased from memory.

This, of course, would not be the case. The school was given five key issues to address, including:

- eradicating inadequate teaching
- raising attainment in maths, reading and writing
- giving children in EYFS (Early Years Foundation Stage) a better start to their education
- raising standards of behaviour and safety
- improving the quality of leadership.

The reality was that the report had to be published and, cynically, just as the school broke for summer, making it more difficult to challenge the findings. The longer it went unchallenged, the more the report wording and judgements would become immortalised.

The first 90 days: rapid impact plans

For reasons already explained, we recognised that our areas for improvement would not be addressed simply by tightening accountability or adopting 'soldier-style' leadership tactics – in other words, mowing down the staff and replacing them with new recruits. We had to focus in equal measure on our core values, pedagogy, leadership of learning and curriculum design. Creating a climate for deep learning to flourish would be as much about social capital and co-constructing a new future as it would be about testing outcomes.

We also knew that lasting improvement would depend on our success in building teams, networks and 'followers' – in other words, an invested learning community where interdependence and growth occurs because everyone sees themselves as investors, owners and creators of change. To achieve this we had to establish a climate of trust, where mistake-making and risk-taking were not only tolerated but actively encouraged. This counterintuitive approach meant finding the balance between strategy – the transformation plan, deadlines, the data dashboard and professional development – and what we called 'deep seeking meaning'. By this, I mean our core purpose, our reasons for change, our 'why'. Ownership and belonging come from and lead to deeper levels of conversation and mutual investment in a school's values and beliefs. Leadership is demonstrated not by mandating change but by creating a climate where change flourishes. As Peter Block highlights in his book *Community*, 'What makes community building so complex is that it occurs in an infinite number of small steps.'

The challenge was tempering experience of knowing what needed to be done with a conscious effort to step back to reflect, refine and begin the conversations that would engage others in the task ahead. We wanted to create uplift, so that the transition between old and new was managed through a collective approach of building social capital, avoiding the vicious cycle of resistance stalling momentum. We recognised a need to cultivate networks amongst staff, build leadership followers and forge strong relationships. At a time when our instinct was to push, pull or even drag change, through our experience we knew that the best solution was to lead through attraction, building alliances and enhancing credibility.

The period from the inspectors leaving the building until the last day of summer term was 40 working days. By the end of July 2014, Foxfield Primary School was already unrecognisable from the school that Ofsted visited in May. While that sense of injustice still burned, the changes we needed to make meant that we had to look ahead instead of backwards. So much needed to be done, we had neither the time nor the energy to dwell on what had happened. We needed to create a transformation culture where change was seen as a positive rather than negative consequence. People accepted that the school was not in good shape but translating this into meaningful action required both skill and understanding.

Two dominant emotions drove change in this space between the inspection itself and the final report publication. One was a sense of injustice that the inspection system was disingenuous to those school leaders (me!) prepared to risk all by choosing to work in schools destined for a poor inspection outcome. This view was tempered by a more rational stance that pupils were actually being failed and inspectors had little choice. However, the incredulity fuelled a desire to prove people wrong and rewrite the narrative. The second prevailing emotion was faith, trust and belief that change would happen rapidly and create a legacy and a vision for learning.

Early wins

The initial period of transformation required early wins. These build confidence, create a 'can do' climate and establish trust. They also enhance the credibility of leaders. As people learn to trust, these early wins mobilise and galvanise teams to believe in a cause, which ultimately enables greater leverage and influence. However, do not confuse early wins with easy wins. Early wins require leaders to put 'whys' before 'whats' and 'hows' (see Chapter 6, p.71, for more about the affective learning domain). Broken schools often have broken cultures and the values base for leadership and decision-making can be fractured.

Some broken schools are led in the interests of the headteacher, some for the staff or parents, and others a combination of all. Therefore, significant emphasis should be placed on establishing a values base where children come first. Questions we asked included:

- Is values education an explicit element of our curriculum?
- Do staff model the school's positive values in their behaviour?
- Is there a focus on creating and maintaining positive relationships?
- Is the school environment happy, calm and purposeful?
- Is reflection utilised as a key tool in thinking and learning?
- Is an emphasis on caring for self and others supporting high staff morale?
- Above all, can we say that a key focus of our curriculum and work is the formation of caring, civil and well-educated people?

We decided that our 'why' was to develop pupils and staff learning through deep collaboration. As examples of this, we established an open-door policy across the school, so that staff, leaders, pupils and visitors were given licence to learn from each other. Open doors didn't just mean classrooms either – we took the locks from leaders' office spaces and created a new shared 'leadership suite' – accessible to everyone – right in the heart of the school. The headteacher's office moved from a security-protected corridor into the centre of the school, so that parents, staff and pupils could *see* the leadership. Where previously pupils were unable to get past the code, now they could wander in and say hello – a simple change with a big impact.

Strategy

Early wins also require strategy. Our strategy was informed by a clear and consistent vision for learning that we wanted to develop across the school. This required a shift of focus to what matters most – those things that actually have the biggest impact on learning – and sweeping aside what doesn't. This included:

- observing lessons
- coaching teachers and introducing peer evaluation
- enhancing professional development
- using data wisely
- continuously evaluating teaching.

To achieve this quickly required a targeted approach, where evidence (instructional levers) was aligned with relationships (cultural levers).

Instructional levers

1 Evidence-based – defines the roadmap based on the needs of pupils.

2 Observation and feedback – provides all teachers with professional 1:1 coaching that increases their effectiveness.

3 Quality curriculum planning – connects learning with skills and purpose.

4 Professional development – strengthens both culture and vision for learning.

Cultural levers

1 Pupil culture – building resilience, collaboration and belief in excellence.

2 Staff culture – focused on discretionary effort, teamwork and collaboration.

3 Leadership culture – narrowing the hierarchy gradient, instilling belief in the vision for learning across the school.

Transformation plans

We created transformation plans that highlighted all of the areas for improvement that Ofsted identified, alongside our own core priorities for change. These included:

- The learning environment – how classrooms and spaces support the organisation of learning and reflect our shared standards for quality of learning outcomes.
- Curriculum expectations – including mapping key skills and knowledge, how topic choices lead to personal development, connecting learning to the wider world and supporting pupils in connecting learning between subject areas.
- Assessment (both formative and summative) – understanding pupils' starting points, enabling continuous assessment and feedback to drive learning priorities, giving pupils the tools to evaluate their own learning and making sure feedback is purposeful.
- Core teaching and learning expectations – developing a common framework for learning where questioning, scaffolding, modelling and application of skills lead to deep understanding of learning concepts.
- Behaviour leadership – helping pupils develop self-efficacy, confidence and the skills to self-regulate learning behaviours.

The transformation plans mapped out, week by week, our key focus areas and specific actions required by staff, and identified training and professional development and also how we would evaluate the impact of success. Critically, the plans were action- and belief-focused. If beliefs change over time, actions can have immediate impact. We wanted transformation planning to focus on both the Ofsted key issues and also on what we believed would have the most positive impact on shaping a school-wide culture that placed excellence and greater depth learning at the very heart of everything we did. Photos 1 and 2 show learning displays that demonstrate how we placed excellence at the centre of our school culture.

We wanted quality learning to be defined not just as an outcome based on limited judgements, but as one where skills are inter-disciplinary, skilfully woven across learning domains and subjects, interdependent on social learning. Our aim was for learning and leadership to be centred not around the performance but around the multiple rehearsals and marginal gains. Depth and quality of learning, we argued, is about opportunity *and* struggle. Greater-depth learning is a process, not an outcome, and it comes from multiple opportunities to fail and learn from error. It is predicated on rich learning experiences that connect the whats and hows with the whys. Greater-depth learning has a values base and a language associated with risk-taking, growth mindset and challenge. It is exactly what Sir Michael Barber described as far back as 2010, in his lecture 'The Prospects for Global Education Reform', when he spoke of knowledge, skills and thinking being worthless unless we give pupils an ethical underpinning to connect these three things, alongside opportunities to lead and transform the world. To achieve and embed this approach at Foxfield, we developed a strategy that established the following:

1   A shared approach to the learning environment

In establishing a school-wide culture that says 'this place feels different', for both staff and pupils, it was important to bring a sense of consistency and order within a school; improving the learning environment was therefore the first change we made. The focus was to ensure that:

- the learning environment provided the visual reference for what the school valued
- it dictated the school-wide expectation for learning
- we provided models to both staff and children about how we learned.

2   Consistency in learning

Once we knew where teaching strengths and areas for development lay, we were next able to design a consistent approach to teaching and learning. Too few schools ensure that leaders are also leaders of learning – another common feature of broken schools.

We ensured that leadership team meetings focused on improving teaching and used a common language linked to learning. Questions to consider included:

- What are our core teaching sequence expectations and how are we planning for these?
- How do we ensure teacher modelling includes explicitly teaching skills and learning dispositions using the approach of 'I do, we do, you do'?
- How are we defining core expectations for high quality learning outcomes?
- Is there a shared understanding of our 'ethic of excellence'?

3   A connected curriculum

This was addressed by ensuring that planning teams used a text, e.g. Macbeth, painting, film or artefact to support them in planning a coherent learning journey that was ambitious, purposeful and predicated on developing quality outcomes. Teams worked together to determine what their outcomes would look like and planned backwards from there. Adults produced models of excellence to share so that children knew what they were aiming for.

Photo 1 *Learning topics were carefully selected to raise expectations and connect knowledge, skills and application*

Photo 2 *An example of collaborative learning which promotes our ethic of excellence*

4   Deep feedback

Assessment of learning became something that pupils were taught to be more engaged with so that peer support and the development of pupil voice in learning led to increased engagement and ownership of learning. We developed language frameworks (see Figure 2) to scaffold pupil responses to feedback and mechanisms to increase peer-to-peer support.

5   Mastery learning (see Chapter 7)

This focused on the quality and depth of the learning journey to ensure that pupils connected knowledge and skills with a bigger cause; deep learners connect what they learn with a reason to learn. They see relationships and patterns and apply skills to a context

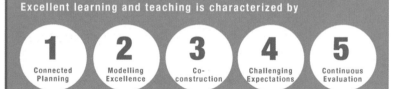

Foxfield Primary School
Teaching & Learning

Foxfield
PRIMARY SCHOOL

"Give children teaching that is determined, energetic and engaging. Hold them to high standards. Expose them to as much as you can, especially the arts. Recognise the reality of race, poverty and social barriers, but make children understand that barriers don't have to limit their lives. Above all, no matter where in the social structure children are coming from, act as if the possibilities are boundless" **Charles Payne (So Much Reform)**

Our Core Teaching and Learning Expectations

Planning
Ensures assessment informs new learning, skills and planned high quality outcomes. Planning weaves across curriculum areas, ensuring learning contexts are rich and linked to moral purpose.

Making Excellence Visible
Connected planning ensures all adults and pupils understand and can see the 'learning journey'; including 'what am I learning?', 'how?' and 'why?'.

Modelling Excellence
Teaching identifies examples of excellence and deconstructs 'what a good one looks like'. Models of quality outcomes are provided visually, broken down and continuously referred to.

Questioning
Promotes discussion, talk for learning, building emotional connections and interest: 'What do you think? 'What does this mean?' 'Why do you think that?' 'How does this link with?'

Learning Environment
Is the invisible teacher. It provides the reference for highest standards, promotes curiosity and charts the learning journey. Environments are always language rich.

Clear Learning Intentions and StS
These are specific, relevant to need and always shared. The StS are processes not outcomes and never limit learning.

Modelling Skills and Strategies
All lessons contain adult modeling and exemplify best practice and excellence from children. Modelling is visible.

Challenge
Learning is challenging. Lessons provide opportunities to apply skills taught to new contexts and reference wider world. Challenge extends thinking beyond class.

Collaboration
Adults and pupils are equally responsible for learning. Learning is designed to be collaborative with peer and adult coaching supporting and enabling success.

Feedback
Feedback is continuous and ever present. Feedback is specific to next steps and provides clear pathways to success. Feedback is an actionable learning dialogue.

Marking
Adults and pupils co-construct new learning through quality marking experiences. Marking is specific & provides next steps. Time is always made for marking responses.

Exit Tickets
Lessons contain multiple opportunities to evaluate and assess learning. Reflections on learning are language rich, collaborative & deepen metacognitive skills.

Excellent learning and teaching is characterized by

1 Connected Planning

2 Modelling Excellence

3 Co-construction

4 Challenging Expectations

5 Continuous Evaluation

Photo 3 *We created standardised expectations to ensure consistency in pedagogy*

where learning can make a difference. Therefore, the importance of curriculum design for providing opportunities to connect learning with the world is imperative.

6 Supportive leadership

We established our core focus on teaching and learning and introduced new leadership expectations. Leadership team agendas became transparent, were shared in advance and focused on impact. The leadership team developed rapid impact plans and weekly impact evaluations linked to the key actions, and governors provided critical support and challenge through a rigorous programme of visits.

Throughout the book, I will revisit these strategy points and demonstrate how we applied them to everything we did in order to radically change not just the Ofsted rating of the school, but also the attitudes and aspirations of staff and pupils.

Our context

Before moving on, it is worth placing into context the two schools in which these stories of improvement are set. First, Woodhill, where I was introduced as their new headteacher from September 2013 after completing my (apprentice) headship at Bannockburn Primary School. (Once again, thank you to Bannockburn governors and thank you Charlie!) And then Foxfield Primary School, which only started working in partnership with Woodhill from April 2014, just as Foxfield was about to be placed in special measures.

It was a unique partnership because both schools were characterised as failing. Because of this, the partnership was viewed (at the time) as unsustainable, even inappropriate, by the Department for Education (DfE). After Foxfield was placed into special measures, three separate DfE officials visited the school, all of them keen to dissolve the partnership so that Foxfield could be forced to join an existing MAT. It was just a matter of when, not if. Each time they visited, however, much to our amusement, they could see an improving school – a special measures school in partnership with a school deemed to be requiring improvement. We took delight in leading learning walks celebrating the high standards, displaying beautiful learning in books and impeccable behaviour. As we walked round, we would quote the Ofsted report that was so damning of the school and its community. It became a game of cat and mouse. We were the proudest special measures school one could hope to be!

The DfE strategy to force Foxfield to join another partnership highlighted more key learning for the education system:

1   School improvement is not always logical.
    The rational action would have been to place Foxfield in partnership with a successful school or trust, but this would have been blind to the (seemingly) irrational context that was Woodhill and Foxfield already in an emerging relationship. In other words, the logical can sometimes be prone to blind spots. To view Foxfield as separate to Woodhill, at a time when the two schools were working well together, would have been the equivalent to analysing bees by studying individual bees rather than examining the whole colony. Although both schools were individually seen as weak, as a collective we were strong.

2   We should never put blind faith in policymakers or an improvement system that lacks experience and maturity.
    Wisdom and experience are always worth more than talk. Too many decisions that affect the lives and livelihoods of others rest in the hands of people who have the capacity to pass tests and appear successful but have no experience of the real world. To truly

understand what made the partnership between Woodhill and Foxfield successful, you had to first understand their communities.

A Woodhill story

Standing proud amongst the high-rise flats flanking three sides of the building, many of which are now identified for demolition as part of an ambitious regeneration project, Woodhill Primary School is in an area that ranks as one of London's most challenged communities in the UK. Serving a population where 70 per cent of children receive free school meals, there is high unemployment and the percentage of families with English as an additional language (EAL) is significantly above the national average. In 2016, 180 pupils either left or joined the school mid-year from a population of just over 500 pupils. Most of these were children new to the UK and didn't have English as their native language.

Built in 1882 for 800 pupils living in 'Lower Woolwich', the opening of Woodhill School was delayed by opposition from residents occupying the large red-brick homes located on 'Little Heath'. Their argument against opening up a new school was that 'the school would be "nearly surrounded by houses which are occupied by a class of persons not likely to send their children to a Board School"' (English Heritage Survey of London, 2012). The middle-class families did not want their nineteenth-century ambiance of suburban, tree-lined Charlton to be spoilt by the sights and sounds of poor people.

The London Board made various concessions before Woodhill Primary School was eventually opened, the main one being that pupils could not pass through the more affluent Wood Street and had to take the longer route in order to come to school. Opponents to the school also insisted that the south facade of the school was constructed in loftier design, including arches and gables, in keeping with the existing stock. Remarkably, classrooms had to be constructed on the darker north side of the building, and boys were housed in the north elevation classrooms so as not to upset the local residents.

Only three generations before, the community had made a significant contribution to the success of a thriving dockyard. Light industry provided a second layer of employment, and retail developments meant that work opportunities were plentiful. The community had an identity, to which it remains loyal and proud.

In the present day, you need only to walk ten minutes north east, crossing the 'lower road', and you are transported into a very different community. With nodding references to its military past, a new development of apartments and family homes is being constructed just a short walk from the new Crossrail development. Built from reclaimed London stock bricks, with geometric, landscaped communal gardens, these apartments, by design, will ensure that the Woodhill community remains locked out of its own back garden. Artisan bakeries, wine bars and delis are all genetically modifying London's smartest new quarter – Woolwich is being reborn. New housing developments sprawl along the river, both east and west, where a new generation of ambitious, twenty-somethings bring very different expectations. Cultural capital is high; community is defined more by coffee shops and gastropubs than by the people who have grown up here, just a short walk away.

It is hard, when crossing over the road into the Royal Arsenal complex, not to think of the families from Woodhill left behind. If the fabric of community is developed one room at a time, so too can it be dismantled in the same way. This is why education is such an important tool in our collective vision for better.

Widening inequality

The stark reality is that poverty, health and housing conditions influence child development as much as – if not more than – education. Policies to reduce early inequalities have been inconsistent and results have been mixed. Although poverty and health inequalities have improved, housing-related problems have worsened significantly. At a time of austerity and cutbacks, we have somehow managed to turn a blind eye to our most vulnerable communities.

Reducing child poverty was declared a national priority in 1999. Child-related benefits rose 60 per cent by 2005, with the steepest increase for parents of children under five. In addition to financial support, government also targeted job-finding support at lone parents – and employment rates increased from 45 per cent to 57 per cent by 2009. As a result, child poverty fell for most of the decade between 2000 and 2010, as did parental worklessness. The recession of 2008 and resulting budget cuts reversed some of this progress, and child poverty has risen since 2010. Nonetheless, over the 20-year period, as a whole, child poverty (after housing costs) still fell three percentage points.

The 2017 *Time For Change* report (Social Mobility Commission) highlighted a concerning trend of gaps widening between advantaged and disadvantaged communities. Most worryingly, we are also encountering a period where education budget cuts and public expenditure are falling consistently over a three-year trend. The combined impact of this means that for the first time since 1911, people born after 2001 are more likely to be worse off than the previous generation. The expectation that each generation would be better off than the previous one is no longer being met.

In Figure 1, we can see the gap in income widen between our richest and poorest communities. The bottom fifth percentile saw their income increase by just over £10 per week in the period following the 2008 recession. During the same period, income for the top fifth per cent rose by just over £300 per week. Within these same households, there are not only inequalities of income but also inequalities of language, social capital and expectation.

In 2013, Paul Marshall edited and published *The Tail*. This marked a serious attempt to challenge the thinking that it could ever be acceptable to set education floor standards for primary-age pupils at 60 per cent (and then 65 per cent). Marshall and other academics argued, essentially, that we are all complicit in the failure of thousands of pupils failing to reach minimum requirements in English and maths. Moreover, we have enough research to categorise who these children are. Many, but not all, come from communities where

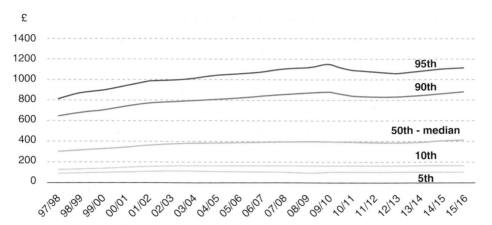

Figure 1 *This graph demonstrates the real weekly household income, after housing costs, in Great Britain from 1997 to 2015/6 (Source: Social Mobility Commission, 2017)*

social and economic deprivation determine the mindset towards achievement and learning. Boys feature more highly than girls and the SEND (special educational needs and disabilities) label is used far too readily to excuse underachievement.

The Tail provides evidence from a range of Western European countries who perform far better than the UK does across all age bands, and questions why this is the case. The book offers an alternative vision in the form of a manifesto, calling for floor standards to be increased to 90 per cent over time. *The Tail* also highlights huge regional differences in provision and outcomes for pupils. It calls for earlier intervention to support child development in a range of areas, including:

- mental health
- language development
- social and emotional growth
- positive parenting
- physical development.

The Tail also highlights the link between school leadership and underachievement, going as far as to say that 'the quality of teaching and leadership in schools is the key factor in raising student achievement'. What typifies these school leaders is their refusal to set the bar lower for any group of pupils. The mantra is clearly one of excellence for all, not some.

However, it is close to impossible for a school serving the most disadvantaged pupils to be evaluated as anything better than good. Fewer than two per cent of schools serving the country's most challenging communities, as measured by poverty indices, are judged outstanding. Research published in the TES (Barker, 2016) confirmed that a family living next to a school rated 'inadequate' by Ofsted is more than 60 per cent more likely to be on a low income than one living next door to an outstanding one. While the reasons for this may be complex, including school admissions policies, the mobility of our poorest pupils and the nature by which school inspection has prioritised pupil outcomes as the measure of success, there can be no denying that poverty has an impact on what kind of school you attend.

In 2017, the proportion of schools receiving an outstanding grade, compared to the true value they add in communities where cultural capital and learning currency is already high, is shocking. In a publication from the Royal Society of Arts called *The Ideal School Exhibition* (2017), they distinguish between schools who 'game' the system versus those 'missionaries' driven by a deeper sense of moral purpose and desire to create lasting cultural change across communities.

The report questions how widespread the problem of schools gaming the accountability system is, how that problem manifests itself and what effect it is having on the character and quality of the education that England's school children are receiving. In the introduction to the report, author Julian Astle describes the pressures of the 'constantly shifting demands of the government's accountability system'. He describes how the risks associated with leadership have 'become so high, with governors and trustees fearing for their schools and headteachers fearing for their jobs, that the task of clearing the latest threshold or hitting the next target has come to dominate almost everything many schools do'.

A Foxfield story

If Woodhill evokes memories from the past, two miles east, Foxfield very much looks out towards the future. A spaceship of a building, spanning multiple levels, it confidently spreads itself wide amongst the narrow-windowed council-built homes. More a Sandbanks beach retreat than a utilitarian primary school, this newly constructed Foxfield building wants you to know it is there. Set halfway up Burrage Road, outward-facing towards the new Royal Arsenal complex and west towards the Canary Wharf, the school is aspirational in every way – except, that is, for the fact that the quality of learning taking place within the building told a very different story in 2014.

Similarly to Woodhill, Foxfield serves a community of high deprivation. The Glyndon estate, on which the school sits, has a history of social and cultural neglect. Reported crime is higher than national levels and funding for public amenities, including libraries and parks, has been eroded over time. Residents feel hard done by and patronised. Both schools have had to come to terms with economic and social disparity, coupled with a crippling poverty of aspiration. Both schools are challenged by cultural neglect, which means that education and learning are not always foremost in families' priorities, the impact of which affects pupils' attitudes towards school and their learning dispositions.

In *Giving Kids a Fair Chance*, James Heckman writes about the kind of future that the families from Foxfield and Woodhill need. He identifies the non-cognitive characteristics that, when nurtured, contribute to social success; these include resilience, perseverance, motivation and self-esteem. IQ is not the reliable indicator of future success that we once thought it was.

Key questions to consider:

1 How much of the immediate response to the Foxfield Primary School inspection outcome was based on planned strategy versus organic improvement?

2 What external barriers to improvement exist in your school and how do you tackle these?

3 What are the cultural levers, including the identified ways of working, shared expectations and beliefs that define how you ensure sustainable school improvement in your school?

If culture and climate are the champions for sustainable improvement, how do we make this visible for everyone to see, feel and internalise? In the next chapter, we look more closely at how the learning environment can be used as an enabler; a model for greater-depth thinking; a silent teacher; and a carefully planned reference point for pupils to help free their working memory by building long-term memory associations.

4 The learning environment

Very little, if any, education research has contributed to the debate about the importance of the learning environment on education outcomes. In fact, there is a fair degree of scepticism about whether it does, indeed, make any difference to standards or the quality of the learning experience at all. Speaking in 2016 during the Teaching Schools Council's review, 'Effective Primary Teaching Practice', Professor David Reynolds went so far as to say that the only evidence that environmental factors affect learning outcomes is based on whether classroom temperatures are conducive to learning and whether pupils have access to water! And yet, within our change plans for both Woodhill and Foxfield, transformation of the learning environment was the first thing we focused on.

Respect means to cherish something in all its forms. The spaces in which we spend most of our time convey important messages about what we value most. They are spiritual as well as physical. We cannot divorce our personal values from their manifestation in our classrooms. What we see, think and feel are the true measure of a values base; we experience this ourselves every time we visit a historic building or place of special interest. For our most disadvantaged pupils, this essential element of education is too often overlooked. When we provide our pupils with the very best, when we show them a future they may not otherwise have access to, we take pupils to a place where new possibilities are revealed. As Bill Strickland argues:

> 'The beauty we've designed into our centre isn't window dressing; it's an essential part of our success. It nourishes the spirit, and until you reach that part of the spirit that isn't touched by cynicism or despair, no change can begin.' (Strickland, 2007)

The learning environment also communicates the inner belief system of teachers and pupils. What we see in the work of pupils or in the way classrooms are set up for learning provides valuable assessment for learning about what is going on inside peoples' minds. But here's the twist: just as we need to ensure that pupils are continuously engaged in a dialogue and surrounded by excellence, so too do leaders need to ensure that staff are engaged in the same process. Ron Berger (2003, p.103) writes that:

> 'The most important assessment that goes on in a school isn't done to students but goes on inside students. Every student walks around with a picture of what is acceptable, what is good enough. Each time he works on something he looks at it and assesses it. Is this good enough? Do I feel comfortable handing this in? Does it meet my standards? Changing assessment at this level

This is 'back to front' planning or, to be more precise, starting with the quality outcome or end point in mind and then working back to teach and model how to get there.

The importance of a high-quality learning environment

Why the spaces that staff and pupils inhabit for much of the day have not formed a greater part of the education standards debate is a worthy question to ask. Companies spend millions of pounds ensuring that identity and brand are enshrined in meticulous detail through colour schemes, spaces and design that define the core purpose of an organisation. In 2009, for example, Google invested huge sums to ensure blue used in its links was the right shade, backed by extensive research into how customers' associated beliefs and values change with subtle changes in colour. Interior design, desirable living and our connection with space has propelled environment to art; it is mood-enhancing, statement-making and life-changing. We connect identity with habitation and living. When we visit a grand hotel or museum, it holds status, conveys importance and carries meaning; we behave differently in these spaces, often rising to the elevated expectation that a building commands. So, what about schools as living spaces? Do classrooms communicate the same messages?

Within a school context, a high-quality learning environment not only sends a clear message that excellence is prized, but it also serves as a multiplier for excellence to be achieved. We are propelled to mimic excellence when we are surrounded by it; psychologically, we defer to the expectations of the environment we find ourselves in – that's what happens in a museum. It is a marginal gain, which communicates the powerful message that high-quality learning is treasured. Learning spaces also provide reference points, connect prior learning with new and offer signposts that scaffold thinking and reasoning. When we model how to use the environment to accelerate learning, we make learning a visible, tangible process. It matters less that walls are decorated with vocabulary, signs and symbols, but more that we are actively using these prompts to develop language and extend thinking and reasoning.

What we did

What connected the failure of both Woodhill and Foxfield was how poor the learning environments were in both schools. Two very different buildings but with equally low expectations – they were tired, scruffy and confused. One was a brand-new, modern design (Foxfield) and the other a Victorian London Board School (Woodhill). Both communicated dysfunction and inconsistency and lacked aspiration.

However, within weeks of the leadership teams getting started, learning spaces at both schools were unrecognisable. This happened quickly, avoiding the blindness we all suffer from being in the same spaces for too long.

- We put in place a deliberate strategy, calculated to connect learning spaces with pedagogy and raise the level of expectation for everyone across the community.

- We specified calming colour schemes, reflective of the natural environment, with fabrics that softened the spaces. This included tactile, hard-wearing learning resources, which, like artefacts in a museum, stimulate curiosity and enquiry.

- We banished brightly-coloured plastics and laminated labels – those disconnected words that, too frequently, adorn learning walls but are never referred to and seem to exist separately from the teaching sequences.

- Computer-generated print was minimised to instil a sense of pride in the art of the handwritten word. This necessitated teachers modelling the same high standard that we expected of pupils.

- We insisted that learning walls and topic tables were introduced to provide visible reference points for pupils to use in lessons, strengthening memory muscle and deepening connections between prior and new learning.

- We also grouped pupils by mixed ability in smaller tables of four so that each child had a 'face partner' and 'shoulder partner' to collaborate with. Pupils were trained to collaborate in teams. This reduced the fear of failure, giving permission for pupils to 'steal' ideas from each other. The language of collaboration was displayed and referred to continuously so that pupils developed the capital and agency to respond to a 'useful learning mistake' or a 'partial agreement'. Sentence stems and speaking frames (see Figure 1) adorned classrooms as visible reminders of the language structures we expected pupils and adults to model with one another. This generated confidence and trust amongst pupils and helped us reframe success away from test culture and towards learning from each other.

- We also increased expectations for how learning topics were celebrated in every class. Topic tables became a staple from the Early Years through to Year 6. They included references to the key enquiry questions that would frame learning outcomes and resources in order to enable greater independence in classroom learning. The rationale was based on the need to make learning outcomes clear from the very outset. We called this 'planning backwards'. This was based on the theory that when pupils connect the skills of learning (whats and hows) with the whys of learning, it deepens the emotional and social connection with the intended learning.

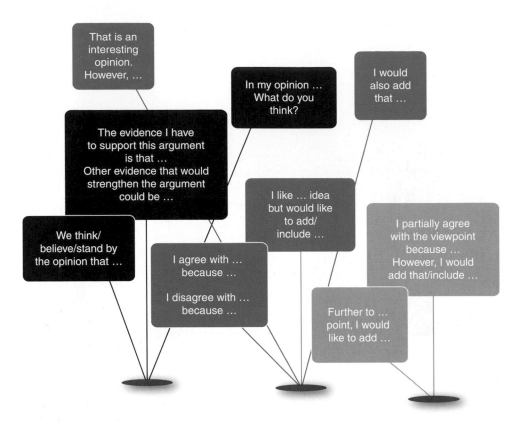

Figure 2 *Speaking frames can increase engagement in learning and improve pupils' ability to reason about their learning*

The visible focus on the learning environment provided an immersive space in which language prompts, reminders, manipulatives and artefacts all served to help pupils make explicit connections between the past, present and future learning. We focused on the following elements of the environment and ensured that all staff understood why these things were important.

Learning walls

The core purpose of a learning wall is to:

- support children's understanding in the process of learning
- provide a visual resource and a reference to scaffold learning
- support current learning and pertinent prior learning
- represent the work in progress and the learning journey steps

- display specific unit modelling for children to access, including children's examples
- help independent learning
- show progress in learning concepts or steps
- model essential concepts, processes and vocabulary.

Photo 4 *Displays should connect stages of learning with high-quality published outcomes*

Interactive displays

Interactive displays are used to:

- encourage children's thinking through enquiry and engagement with learning
- support the development of sustained, active thinking
- provide next steps for learners, e.g. they might form an enquiry task or reinforcement opportunity
- help extend learning beyond the teacher's modelling
- support deeper learning and reinforce key language development.

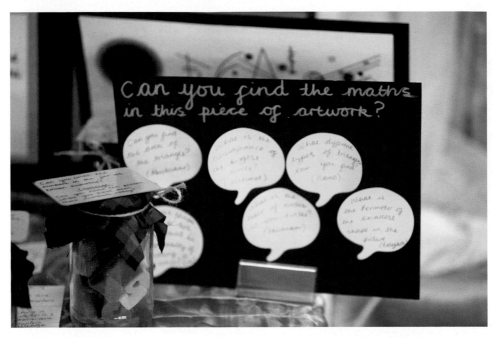

Photo 5 *Displays like this encourage children to interact and support the development of active thinking*

Topic tables and interest tables

Topic tables and interest tables create an instant reference to a learning theme. They promote enquiry and stimulate the senses, drawing learners in by:

- stimulating discussion in lessons linked to a curriculum theme
- generating enthusiasm towards a topic area or an aspect of a topic theme
- providing children with concrete examples or artefacts that prompt thinking
- providing role play and drama opportunities
- displaying learning questions and linking learning across subject areas.

Expansive book corners

Book corners should be inviting, stimulating places to learn and make positive choices about the value of reading. They should:

- be calm, organised and supportive spaces
- use fabrics, cushions and plants to 'soften' the area, making it more inviting
- use key questions, interactive author-focus displays and displays of featured genres to enhance the learning experience for pupils using a book corner well.

Photo 6 *Topic tables create an instant reference to a learning theme*

Photo 7 *Book corners are aspirational spaces that celebrate a love of reading*

Modelled handwriting

We agreed that the expectation for teacher-modelled handwriting would be:

- we use cursive handwriting at all times
- all adults model the cursive script when writing anything for children.

Photo 8 *Cursive handwriting was modelled by teachers and used at all times*

Deepening collaboration

My earliest memory as an NQT was arriving at my new school, in the middle of the summer holidays, to set up my classroom for September. There was no supporting guidance, no shared approach to what my class should include and no induction. I was left alone. I developed a mindset, over time, of 'I knew best'. I retreated into the classroom with 'my' pupils, and the rest of the school did the same. There were no shared planning meetings, no cultural norms about what collaboration meant or required. This was endemic to the profession at the time and allowed a culture of individualism to prevail. Teachers taught by themselves, with classroom doors shut, and feedback seldom penetrated beyond the classroom walls, so ideas about what works best were never shared. I remember creating my own assessment and record-keeping system, which was guarded protectively.

By chance, this was picked up by the LEA (local education authority) advisory teacher on his annual visit to the school as something to share – and when it was, half the staff recoiled to think that we should be open to learning from others. Teachers taught in silos, planned in isolation and, generally, survived rather than thrived by preserving the practice they had grown to know best. This was not a model for learning.

The unintended consequence of implementing a planned approach for lifting expectations through consistent learning environment protocols was that it deepened collaboration between staff across both Woodhill and Foxfield. Without structural opportunities for staff to share, plan, co-construct and exchange ideas about pedagogy, professional collaboration is just a token. Deep collaboration between teachers shapes how people work together; it defines the norms and shared expectations for professional practice. While there is good evidence to support the view that collaboration enhances pupil achievement, the mechanisms for enabling this are not always clear. In our case, choosing to transform learning environments as a core priority brought people together for a shared cause. And because the impact of environment transformation was such a visible example of staff working together – an early win – it very quickly ensured that staff engaged with and became attached to the idea of collaboration. Teachers valued the work they did together because it was so immediate, tangible and dramatic.

Coalition

The importance of school partnerships is much better understood now than in the 1990s. It is now almost universally accepted as the most powerful lever for change. It is distinct and different, however, from professional collaboration – a model where teachers intrinsically value others' ideas, share common beliefs, build coalitions for change, challenge each other professionally and co-construct change. This can only be developed in a climate where it is safe to take risks, be open to giving and receiving feedback and to participate in group tasks focused on curriculum, pedagogy and self-evaluation.

Collaboration was structurally forced upon schools through initiatives like the London Challenge, reinforcing hierarchy and coercion, as great schools rescued the weak (see DfES, 2011 for more information). At Foxfield, the collaboration that transformed the learning environment in wave one of our transformation plan came from design.

- Teachers from Foxfield visited Woodhill and vice versa to 'magpie' ideas; they invested in collective efficacy (a shared belief that together we can make a difference, regardless of the challenge) and took responsibility for collaboration.
- Staff worked in each other's classrooms to create role play areas, ignite reading corners and develop models for excellence in learning walls.
- We also standardised systems for labelling books, ordered new furniture and generated common language prompts for book areas and other elements of the learning spaces. This maximised collaboration but minimised workload.

During this period, relationships strengthened, as did trust. Capacity was given and received in equal measure. Perhaps because Woodhill had been a school designated as 'requires improvement' by Ofsted, there was greater equity between staff across schools. This removed the label of failure, creating agency as staff between schools faced similar challenges. It also helped that staff at Woodhill Primary School, having already been through significant change, were ready to become 'capacity givers' while Foxfield Primary School accepted their need to become 'capacity takers'. And because the transformation of learning spaces had been so successful, it created a template for future collaboration between schools. Effectively, professional collaboration aspired to more than test scores and became aspirational for deeper goals.

Do you remember Marshall's important work, *The Tail*, which we mentioned in Chapter 3? What was clear from that research was that the underachievement in the English education system was complex – dependent on a range of factors, including housing, provision for SEND pupils and regional educational differences. He called for public services to work more closely together, with greater support for families, schools and communities.

However, the education policy published after Marshall's work saw a tightening of accountability rather than a push to increase collaboration between schools. While the government's free school and academy trust policy was designed to release schools from the limiting ambitions of local authorities, promoting a fresh wave of creativity and energy in schools, the reality has seen more schools without the capacity and infrastructure to work together and a disjointed approach to harnessing the potential of the 'system-led' approach to school improvement through the network of NLEs (national leaders of education), teaching schools and regional school commissioners. At a time when we most needed support to capitalise on learning from each other, the system has broken down around us; schools feel more isolated, unsupported and trapped than ever.

When the 'tail' is viewed by local authority groupings, what stands out is huge geographical variations in attainment. Academic performance of pupils, it seems, is still a postcode lottery. Despite serving a community within the bottom quintile, in terms of social disadvantage, the local authority of Tower Hamlets performs significantly better than Knowsley for example. While 103,000 pupils in total are grouped within the tail, if all local authorities performed as well as Tower Hamlets, the number would be only 30,000. The key issue, it seems to me, is believing that children *can* achieve and harnessing the social capital of schools to make sure this happens.

Success for disadvantaged pupils is intrinsically linked to school culture and the ambition of the community to ensure that every pupil achieves the standard of learning to which all pupils are entitled. Great schools are as much about creating a positive climate for learning, underpinned by a belief system that all children can and will achieve – across learning disciplines.

Environment drives behaviour

If culture and climate regulate the ambitions and expectations within a school, what does an environment that supports those ambitions and expectations look like?

I want to argue in the second half of this chapter that repositioning what we value in learning and deepening our collective belief system about how we all learn can have a huge impact in terms of achievement and, perhaps more importantly, how we create a learning community that works for everyone.

Environment *changes* behaviour

In one of the most popular online education clips, Bill Strickland talks about his own journey from disaffected African American to community leader and President of the Manchester Bidwell Corporation in the US. His central argument is that environment drives our behaviours, and how we think, feel and act can be altered by light, space and exposure to beauty. Poverty can dictate whether or not a child has access to an aspirational environment. Poor kids, he argues, 'never get the best treatment; the best food, the best teachers, the best equipment'. (MarionInstituteTV, 2013)

His story is an inspiration: Strickland grew up as a disengaged teenager. Then he met high school art teacher Frank Ross. Ross showed Strickland the power of art, education and community, and instilled in him an interest in working with disadvantaged pupils through an after-school arts programme. In 1968, Strickland launched his own small after-school ceramics course, which grew to become the Manchester Craftsmen's Guild's Youth and Arts Programme, serving public school students via classes in ceramics, design, digital imaging, 3D manufacturing and photography. By 1972, Strickland had also taken over leadership of the Bidwell Training Centre, a struggling job training centre near the Manchester Craftsmen's Guild. He rebuilt the organisation into a job training and vocational centre, in partnership with various Pittsburgh area industry leaders. This is now a nationally accredited and state-licensed adult career training institution, with programmes that range from horticulture to medicine to the culinary arts. 'We partner with industry leaders to develop curriculum specific to their industries,' explains Strickland. 'We have these industry advisory boards that work directly with us. The programs we develop are industry compatible, so as to have a high degree of placement and retention.' Manchester Bidwell's arts education opportunities for public school students are directly connected to this work.

Speaking of the pioneering architectural design of the glass structure that is the Bidwell Training Centre, Strickland states, 'we have never had a broken window, no graffiti, no theft, no drugs, not one police call in 26 years. Everywhere your eye turns in this school there is something beautiful looking back at you. This is quite deliberate. We have $200,000 in art work displayed with no anti-theft system on the art. We haven't lost a screw driver in

26 years. Beautiful buildings create beautiful people. If you build these kind of buildings you get world class results.'

The learning environment became an immediate focus of attention at both Woodhill and Foxfield, because we wanted to:

1   Show our pupils and community that learning was something we prized and cherished above all else.

2   Expose pupils to the very best we could give them in order to raise collective aspirations.

We also wanted to send a message to the community that change was afoot, that something exciting was happening – something so special that you could see it, touch it and feel it. We wanted the messages we were delivering about our shared values to become tangible. For too long, pupils at both schools had been treated to the worst of what a school can offer. Torn chairs, broken furniture, dirty plastic learning materials. The community was ambivalent to the low expectations communicated from messy book corners and badly photocopied and smudged newsletters. From now on, everything we did was going to give the message that only the very best would do. This is what we meant by environment serving as a silent teacher. It supports the messages about a school's ethos, what is valued and how this manifests. After all:

> 'The beauty we've designed into our centre isn't window dressing; it's an essential part of our success. It nourishes the spirit, and until you reach that part of the spirit that isn't touched by cynicism or despair, no change can begin.' (Bill Strickland, 2007)

Transforming the Woodhill environment

The new leadership that entered Woodhill Primary School in July 2013 had a mammoth task. Nothing about the building or its classrooms communicated the values or aspirations that the children deserved. The building was dirty, furniture was torn and shabby, and dull classrooms with flaking paintwork were wholly uninspiring. Too many learning resources were plastic and 'Disney-fied'. It communicated not just low expectations but also an apathy towards teaching and learning that transcended the whole community. There were buckled coat pegs, pupil names scratched on with ballpoint pens, plastic pencil pots with half-chewed pencils. Outdoor play spaces were overgrown with weeds and bins were left unemptied. Along corridors, displays of children's learning lacked imagination and creativity. Some displays were torn and contained minimum standards of learning rather than the very best, and there was no sense of consistency between learning spaces.

By the end of the 2013 six-week summer break, even before pupils entered, the whole school had undergone a transformation. This included:

- a thorough deep clean of the school (including carpets, windows, blinds, walls, outdoor learning spaces, halls and corridors)
- new, high-quality wooden classroom furniture for every room
- re-backing all display boards in calming, neutral colours to create a consistent feel to the school
- identifying non-negotiables for all learning spaces
- creating example displays around the main corridors to model expectations for presenting pupils' best learning.

During the first two days that pupils were in school, staff emphasised heavily that the school was different, felt different, looked different. Children wrote letters home to families explaining how they felt in the spaces and the intended impact that we hoped this would have. They deserved the best, were given the best and they responded to the challenge to be the best. Environment drives behaviour.

A second set of actions concerned establishing a clear vision with a definitive road map to ensure that the learning environment was being used effectively to promote quality learning experiences. This included:

- displaying learning environment key consistencies for staff to use as a reference point
- identifying and communicating key expectations for teaching sequences
- developing a common language for learning that connected the environment with pupils' outcomes.

The shape of staff training concentrated on:

- defining quality learning and how the environment makes this visible
- identifying key teaching sequences, which maximise success in lessons
- describing common expectations for learning outcomes
- agreeing leadership behaviours and actions that make all of this happen.

Leadership provided as many visual references to great learning spaces as we possibly could so that teachers could see the collective expectations. We also published core expectations posters for what every learning environment needed to include. The focus on learning environment was a significant amount of work, but gave the school community a shared responsibility for the organisation of learning. It provided a tangible and noticeable cultural shift, which was felt by all. Pupils began to understand and appreciate how the

CORE VALUES

RESILIENCE
LOVE
COLLABORATION
INTEGRITY
KINDNESS
FORGIVENESS
FRIENDSHIP
RESPONSIBILITY
RESPECT
EXCELLENCE
EFFORT

Photo 9 *Core values posters reminded pupils of our expectations*

building was a place of aspiration and inspiration. This enabled pupils, staff and visitors to gain insight into the learning going on in classrooms – learning in progress as well as the finished product. Achievements were celebrated through learning displays and the pride taken in the learning journey towards excellence. Pupils developed a deeper understanding about how classroom environments provide an interactive resource to support teaching, learning and assessment effectively – for example, providing prompts, models, good examples and information that children can use to support their learning on a daily basis. Pupils were encouraged to use spaces effectively by making reference to the models and examples of learning provided, and to ensure that these were regularly updated so as not to become 'wallpaper'. Spaces became empowering. They helped regulate the climate. They were reflective of the breadth of curriculum provision, expectations for deep rather than shallow learning, and the support and challenge provided so that all pupils achieve well. They promoted shared responsibility, respect for each other's learning and a sense of ownership of learning.

By the end of the autumn term in 2013, there was already a cultural shift and belief system about excellence, pupil learning and high standards. It came not from a monitoring framework but because teachers, pupils and parents felt it all around the building.

Table 5 Teachers used a framework they created to evaluate the learning environment

	Emerging	Developing	Highly accomplished	Embedded excellence
Learning environment	The environment is organised and purposeful. Learning environments identify key areas within classrooms including book corners, learning walls, topic tables and curriculum areas. Pupil books and other resources are stored neatly in an organised way. Resources are clearly labelled.	Learning environments are stimulating, well organised and contain evidence of high expectations. This can be identified through the organisation of resources, the quality of learning on display and through quality of modelling.	The learning environment is aspirational, with every area providing models of excellence. Key vocabulary, examples of modelling and learning walls reflect the highest expectations and are used by pupils to enhance learning.	The learning environment is an inspirational place to learn. There is multiple evidence that the environment is used as a resource to enhance learning, build collaboration and promote the school's values.

When Ofsted arrived just ten weeks after the school embarked on a journey that placed environment high on the list of priorities, they identified that leadership had…

'firmly set the school on an improving course. This has inspired and raised the expectations, skills and accountability of senior leaders, staff and governors. Rapid and successful action is well underway to improve significant aspects of the school's work, including significant refurbishment of the school to improve the learning environment, staff training to increase leadership capacity, improvements in behaviour and not least, changes in the culture and ethos in the school and its status in the community.' (Ofsted, 2013)

As a staff, we devised a framework to define what we valued in schools at different levels. The learning environment was one theme. Teachers used this as a guide to peer-evaluate how they felt their own classrooms reflected the whole-school expectations.

Defining expectations

Too few schools understand or give the learning environment equal status alongside planning and teaching, leaving it as an optional add-on. As we have seen, when developed effectively, the spaces children learn in have the potential to transform the way pupils learn, at the same time as sending powerful messages about school expectations, values and beliefs. A connected approach to planning for high-quality learning places environment at the centre of learning and shifts the focus of learning away from surface learning towards deeper levels of understanding. Matthew Syed (2011) refers to 'social multipliers'; Daniel Coyle (2010) describes 'ignition' – both are references to the opportunities or conditions that inspire excellence. These could also be described as the culture and climate created in an organisation that value specific skills or attitudes leading to success. The learning environment is an extraordinary multiplier for expertise and should be given higher priority when creating a school-wide pedagogical framework. Here's why:

Tuning in

Just as in an art gallery or museum exhibition, quality learning spaces inspire curiosity across learning domains – often raising questions and provoking deeper enquiry.

Integrated learning

Learning walls or modelled displays can make the 'whole' learning concept visible and provide a rich context for learning. This helps pupils see where the intended learning aspires to be.

Organising information

The environment builds neuroplasticity. When pupils can make physical connections between the learning spaces (e.g. learning walls) and learning concepts, this helps push working-memory learning into long-term memory, freeing up learning slots and increasing cognitive bandwidth.

Raising aspiration

Outstanding classrooms model the expectation required for excellence to be reached. They also provide reference points to help pupils develop learning strategies like reasoning skills.

It is hard to separate the environment from teaching or planning – it communicates more than just the learning content. It represents the blending of content and pedagogy so that an understanding of how learning is organised, represented and adapted is made visible. There is also a link between mastery learning and how the environment is used as a resource for challenging pupils to gain deeper levels of understanding. When connected to a learning philosophy, the environment can:

- provide a framework to help pupils organise sequences of learning
- build conceptual understanding so that the 'why' of learning is better understood
- encourage deeper levels of reflection
- help learners make sense of the world around them.

The following questions are a useful starting point in helping school leaders audit provision:

1 Does our school have a clear vision for how the environment is used to promote learning?

2 How do the spaces within our school promote curiosity, pedagogy and excellence?

3 What key messages do our school learning environments provide?

4 How effectively do learning environments model expertise?

What started off as a focus on environment moved quickly into planning, pedagogy and curriculum.

Key questions to consider:

1 What messages do your classrooms and spaces communicate about what you value most or least?

2 Which spaces within your school are you most proud of and least proud of? Which parts of your school do you spend most and least time in? What does this tell you?

3 How does your learning environment communicate your whole-school vision and expectations?

4 How do classroom learning environments improve the quality of learning and how do you really know this?

5 How do learning displays celebrate the journey of learning as well as the finished outcomes of learning?

Schools are complex places and bound by relationships. The notion that we can measure everything can distort the reality of what great schools are doing to cultivate and foster improvements. We are building an argument for deepening collaboration between teachers and moving away from hierarchical approaches to planned school improvement. In the next chapter, we look more closely at climate and culture and consider how we might find ways to celebrate their impact in schools.

5 Climate and culture

What typifies a school as a *learning community* is the sense of pride and ambition that acknowledges the need to co-create excellence, designing an alternative future that focuses on the wellbeing of all. Central to Woodhill and Foxfield's success has been the relentless focus on developing learning characteristics, giving children a language for learning that enables young people to excel. There may be some things beyond the school walls that we cannot change, but there is plenty inside that we can.

Climate rules

Unsurprisingly, both Foxfield and Woodhill had lost sight of their core purpose in serving vulnerable communities by the time the inspectors came – and for different reasons. If culture is determined by our actions, and climate by how it feels to belong, it was very hard to define either school by community or belonging. It is the sense of belonging that defines community and, for many pupils and families, this was absent. As we've seen, the inspection that placed Foxfield in special measures highlighted how the 'curriculum was reduced to revising literacy and numeracy skills' and how pupils '[lost] concentration, and [distracted] others from learning. Young children [squabbled], [found] it hard to share resources or take turns.' (Ofsted, 2014) Rebuilding our learning community was the defining challenge.

It started by developing a shared understanding of culture and climate. Our goal was to nurture the ten per cent discretionary effort within teams that we felt could be the difference for our community. We wanted to focus on staff behaviours first in order to create consistency – not just for teaching and learning or the learning environment, but also within approaches to planning lessons, working collaboratively and building teams.

We created culture and climate rubrics to highlight core staff behaviours, which helped focus collective and individual responsibility for creating an enabling environment. Staff worked in teams to evaluate where culture and climate enabled team successes. These were celebrated publically in briefing notices and through our staff shout-out notices. This had an unintended consequence, which helped staff value the small things as having a more significant impact than the rapid completion of multiple tasks.

With so much to do after the inspection, the risk could have been to view improvement via tick-lists. Paying attention to specific behaviours, outlined in the rubrics, helped staff view the world through the eyes of an artist, where cultural change was measured not

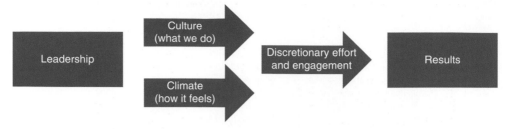

Figure 3 *Leadership can be seen as critical but indirect*

through the completion of hours in work, but by the impact of relationships and our ability to notice and celebrate the marginal gains.

By valuing staff interdependence, fostering a climate where depth of collective focus was prized more highly than initiative busyness, we made the link between actions and core values a tangible one. Immersion and investment in each other helped us narrow the gaps in behaviours that required further attention. We held meetings where culture and climate became barometers for success instead of task completion. We devised postcards that were posted home to staff where discretionary effort had been noticed. Leadership action plans contained explicit references attending to culture and climate. Senior leadership team meetings began by sharing the too-often-untold stories championing children's achievements in the broadest possible way.

The impact of climate on children

Often lost within the work we do are the children whose learning achievements do not easily fit with a national framework. We spend less time celebrating the incremental successes of pupils with complex needs and more time asking why they are not reaching national standards. While the Rochford Review (2016) recognises that age-related expectations are not an appropriate measure of progress for a significant proportion of pupils in our schools, at national standards reporting level schools are never asked about the cognitive development or progress of our most complex pupils when it comes to reporting data. Why? The risk of this causes institutional bias, where the narrative of high performance ignores the reality of marginal gains in schools who are working hard to recalibrate what progress and achievement *really* look like for pupils learning significantly below age-related expectations.

To combat this, we created key performance indicators that broke down achievement into smaller chunks, allowing us to measure 'small data'. This included personal achievements linked to children's individual needs. We wanted our teachers to be experts in meeting the needs for every child.

Table 6 Culture and climate rubrics were created to focus responsibility for creating an enabling environment

	Emerging	Developing	Highly accomplished	Embedded excellence
Relationships with others	Relationships are positive or are improving. There is recognition that school improvement is dependent on building professional relationships with all members of the school community.	Day-to-day relationships are good and support school improvement. Communication is good amongst teams and professional differences are generally managed well.	Relationships across all groups within the class and school community are excellent and build a climate of trust. Immediate teams are clear about leadership through relationships and model expected behaviours well. Difficulties and challenges are always managed professionally.	Relationships with others are exemplary. Positive behaviours are modelled continuously and professionally. This has a positive impact across the school, beyond immediate teams. Leadership through relationships is embedded and champions the mantra 'this is how we do things around here'.
Quality of planning (the learning journey)	Planning meets national curriculum requirements and school policies. Some learning experiences capitalise on local context and learners' interests.	Planning provides a good curriculum experience, which is broad, balanced and links across subjects. Outcomes are of a good standard. Good use is made of trips, visits and the local context to provide a stimulus for learning.	Curriculum planning offers an excellent provision and leads to pupils reaching high standards in a range of areas. Learning journeys are planned well and are reflected in the learning environment, as well as pupils' books. Links with the local and wider community are excellent and used well to enhance learning experiences.	Class planning leads to an enhanced, high-quality learning experience. Planning maximises freedoms to innovate and inspire learners. Learning journeys are carefully planned and consistently include models of excellence for pupils to see and in advance of learning experiences. Links with the local and wider community are ambitious and broaden pupils' experiences well beyond the school.

Table 6 (continued)

	Emerging	Developing	Highly accomplished	Embedded excellence
Support for teams	There is a desire to belong to the team and informal support provided benefits colleagues. Planning is shared across the team and ensures all teachers are prepared for lessons.	Good relationships and mutual support within school teams enhance provision and quality of teaching and learning. Lesson resources and planning are shared well, which leads to a consistency in practice across the team.	Strong and focused team support leads to improved outcomes and/or rapid improvement within teams. Planning is excellent and a climate of openness welcomes feedback and self-evaluation.	High-quality teamwork ensures team systems are embedded. Planning and professional discussion are focused on achievement and sustaining school strengths.
Modelling excellence	Teaching behaviours and practice demonstrate potential and meet school expectations. Areas of excellence to share have been identified for the future.	Teaching demonstrates examples of innovative practice and this is being shared with other colleagues, with a positive impact on learning. Some practices are being included in CPD (continuing professional development).	Teaching is consistently innovative and creative. Practice is regularly shared with other colleagues. This is improving the learning of others across the staff.	Teaching is recognised as cutting-edge, in both thinking and practice. Practices and behaviours are shaping policy in key areas and inspiring staff. There is evidence of innovation enhancing pedagogy.
Ability to reflect	There is a willingness to reflect on teaching practice and an improving trajectory of practice in key areas. Action points linked to teaching evaluations are followed up.	Teacher reflection leads to improvement in quality of teaching and increased ambition to achieve excellence. There is good evidence of self-direction of CPD and an enthusiastic response to feedback.	Teaching is ambitious and continuously seeking improvements. The teacher is hungry to improve and actively seeks feedback wherever possible. Engagement in research and development is improving practice and this is leading to new practices or rapid improvements in key areas.	Teaching flourishes because of an established climate of reflection and improvement. Reflection improves the practice of self and others and connects with the school's leadership of teaching and learning. All staff connected with the class benefit from opportunities to reflect and share new ideas.

Engagement with R&D	Teaching responds to new initiatives and puts policy into practice. Some decisions relating to teaching and learning are based on evidence and identification of best practice.	There is some staff engagement with research but mainly through external courses. This is improving practice in the classroom and is shared with other colleagues. Wider reading and engagement in R&D is beginning to influence thinking of self and others in the team.	Engagement in research and development is developing and improving practice. Implications from key research initiatives are discussed widely and used where appropriate. Using evidence to inform decision-making is a strong feature of practice and is shared with SLT (senior leadership team), informing school development planning.	There is a systematic engagement in research and a desire to share JPD (joint practice development) and appreciative enquiry. Evidence of impact includes sharing learning in research briefings and contributing well to the CPD of other colleagues (within and beyond school). Evidence-informed decision-making is strongly embedded into systems.
Leadership of change	Change and school improvement initiatives are generally viewed positively. School expectations and policies are implemented. There is some recognition that school improvement necessitates continuous change and revision of expectations.	Change is viewed positively and generally embraced. There is support for change-management processes and willingness to be flexible. There is strong recognition of changing educational landscape and a willingness to engage in discussion about this.	There is good leadership of change and a desire to continuously improve teaching and school-wide practice. Teaching offers strong support for others in change management, including a willingness to trial initiatives or support policy development. This has a positive impact on outcomes for pupils.	In every aspect, there is strong recognition that our work focuses on improving outcomes for children in our locality. Change is embraced and challenged professionally. There is a desire to support other schools in change management and a recognition that continuous improvement benefits the children across our school and also those in other schools.

The impact of the key performance indictors for achievement were dramatic.

- Teachers began to know pupils better, built stronger relationships and were clearer about meeting pupils' needs within the mainstream setting of a classroom.

- Pupils began to demonstrate more positive attitudes towards learning and were better able to connect learning skills beyond school. Critically, by adopting a 'small data' approach to assessing pupils with complex needs, we became much better able to celebrate their individual successes. For example, Child X may not be toilet-trained, but to recognise the need to sit on a toilet is a significant achievement. This is a success worthy of championing.

- We also devised systems so that teachers could celebrate teaching successes or marginal gains across the school where impact was being felt most strongly. Staffrooms contained 'Staff Shout Out' displays as a way of celebrating each other's professional learning (see Photo 10, p. 65).

- Staff learning postcards were sent home to staff where we noticed discretionary effort or where positive learning behaviours had been modelled especially well.

- Peer-to-peer Lesson Study was introduced as a tool for supporting professional development, by way of reducing the fear of 'inspection' as the one golf club approach to school improvement.

- Feedback from NQTs and middle leaders became a focus for governors to triangulate evidence bottom-up rather than top-down. It pulled apart the potential for hierarchy blind spots and challenged assumptions about how learning in lessons should be organised. It led to a whole-school focus on 'greater depth learning', sparked by an NQT who brilliantly noticed an 'incidental moment' from the corner of his eye. It is the permission to lead that transforms schools and sparks learning revolutions – and not an overreliance on accountability.

In turn, this built deeper trust and made the tough professional conversations easier, not harder. By noticing the smallest acts of kindness, all rooted in the value of relationships, staff gave more and grew deeper connections with each other. We gave more time to parents and commitment to collaboratively problem-solving the daily challenges of school life. Making time to write a good news notice, returning a phone call or making time for an anxious parent began to build a community where children came first. We defined this, we codified what it meant and we co-constructed the behaviours that we wanted all staff to exemplify. Inspiring teachers demonstrate several characteristics that are embedded in their daily practice. These include:

- valuing children as individuals
- use of praise for effort

- demonstrating warmth and empathy
- showing respect for pupils.

These are teachers who create climates for learning that strengthen confidence and motivation amongst learners. Fear of failure is replaced by mutual appreciation, collaboration between pupils and investment in each other's triumphs and disasters. In essence, it is the climate and culture created in classrooms that determine outcomes for young people, and this is what drove both Foxfield and Woodhill to succeed.

Photo 10 *Shout-out boards in staffrooms allow staff to recognise their colleagues' successes*

Lessons worth behaving for

The mindset that some pupils are more able to succeed than others or that dysfunctional families are the cause of society's ills is pervasive and limits beliefs. Many will have witnessed the staffroom conversations where blame is attached to the tricky pupil and the implications that this can have in creating 'group think'. Schools have specific triggers, again rooted in culture and climate, which, left unchallenged, erode possibilities. Schools can 'self-diagnose' these, locating the problem away from school. This can manifest in the language used by teachers to legitimise or confirm a belief. For example, 'Child X has never been able to…' or '… the family has always been a problem'. At Woodhill Primary School, for example, staff initially struggled to make the connection between their own low expectations for certain children and the consequential behaviours that pupils exhibited. Transitions between playground and classroom were problematic, not because pupils could not line up or walk calmly back to class, but because staff were frequently late to arrive at the playground or tolerated disruptive behaviour from specific pupils. Similarly, behaviour in lessons was poor because teaching was unstructured and lacked engagement. Unsurprisingly, when Woodhill Primary School was inspected in 2013, inspectors reported that:

> 'Lessons do not fully engage or challenge pupils, the approach to learning of a minority of pupils is not as positive as it should be and they become inattentive and distracted from their tasks which hampers their learning.' (Ofsted, 2013)

We created checklists for staff to give clarity to teachers and create consistency. These concentrated on the core behaviours we wanted to address quickly in order to create a climate of safety and calmness. We codified this as 'The Woodhill Way'. The language was simple, structured and easy to refer to. This generated a scripted approach to tackling the most common misdemeanors, giving staff a framework to work from. It was deliberately instructional but designed to secure the baseline for minimum expectations. This is what football managers might refer to as 'building from the back'.

Simultaneously, we made the link between staff behaviours and outcomes for pupils by creating an audit tool for staff to measure cultural levers and positive learning behaviours. They included relationship-building, how adults modelled traits and behaviours associated with warmth, and also how teachers connected planning with pupils' interests. Our thinking was that lessons should be worthy of pupils' engagement.

There is often a perception gap between what we think about our learning and what our pupils really know. The Australian Institute for Teaching and School Leadership (2016) surveyed thousands of young people in schools across Australia and found that

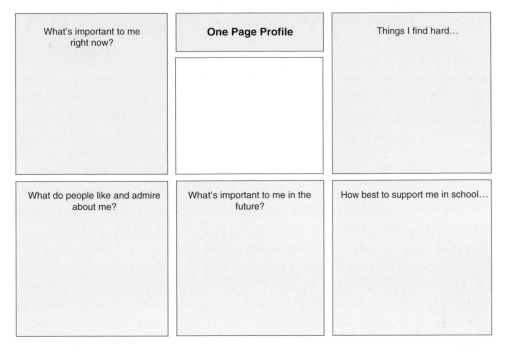

| What's important to me right now? | **One Page Profile** | Things I find hard… |
| What do people like and admire about me? | What's important to me in the future? | How best to support me in school… |

Figure 4 *The 'one page profile' was created to help us find out more about each child*

38 per cent of students said they were bored at school, compared to just seven per cent of teachers who felt that students were bored. Most worryingly, only four per cent of pupils said that school helped them become the person they wanted to be, compared to 30 per cent of their teachers. In order to close this perception gap, we have to create a climate where pupil voice is heard more loudly. At Woodhill, this guided us towards creating simple profiles for children to help us identify their likes, dislikes, hopes and fears.

The simple act of sitting down with children one by one, asking them about family, friends, needs and desires, had a huge impact on shifting the balance of power for learning towards pupils. This strengthened relationships between staff and children and also generated trust between families and school. The information was recorded in pupils' One Page Profiles (see Figure 4). When Ofsted returned to Woodhill in 2016, they reported that:

> *'Pupils' personal development and welfare are outstanding… A strength of the school is the warm relationships between pupils and staff. Pupils respond well to challenging activities… classrooms have a strong productive atmosphere in which pupils enjoy their learning.'*
> *(Ofsted, 2016)*

Table 7 Teachers used behaviour for learning checklists to create consistency

Focus question	Action points
Does class have clear routines that are set in stone? • meeting and greeting/saying goodbye at end of day (both teacher and children) • lining up (spacing and order) • entering & leaving classroom/holding doors open • movement around school (e.g. use of passes/noise level expectations/greeting visitors) • calling to carpet/stopping to listen/working in collaboration/turn-taking • expectations for pupil talk displayed (e.g. what makes a good talk partner) • transitions between lessons • giving out resources/storage of resources	
Does learning environment communicate high expectations? • rules and values clearly displayed and referred to • all areas of classroom clearly defined and labelled • table resources stored neatly using table trays • pupil books organised, accessible & stored in specific areas • teacher resources organised and stored neatly • adult modelling of expectations of the highest standard	
Do adults model quality relationships? • always using positive body language and tone when communicating • always using praise and noticing good behaviour • catching children being good and commenting on this • sharing successes of children with other staff/children/families • expressing empathy/emotions linked to values during significant learning experiences • regularly referencing values during learning time • modelling how to learn as well as teaching curriculum content (e.g. taking turns/sharing resources/talking partners) • using other adults to model relationships during learning tasks	
Do we know our children's personalities and interests? • names of children, likes and dislikes, know something special about them (e.g. birthdays, occasions, family composition) • asks genuine questions to understand children as individuals (seeks to understand) • always follows up on children's requests/questions/comments with sincerity (e.g. after lessons or during break times) • praises significant achievements in a range of areas (not just literacy and numeracy) • spends time with children outside of classroom (e.g. lunch hall/playground)	

Focus question	Action points
Are we investing in relationships? • regular communication with families in a range of contexts including celebrating successes in class • visible around the school before and after school for parents to contact • uses circle time, snack times, informal times to model relationships and references values • plans success criteria that include social skills as well as curriculum content • notices unusual or out-of-character behaviour and always follows up with family or staff	
Does curriculum and learning time meet pupils' individual needs? • teachers audit class profile of skills and needs before deciding on topic choices • children involved in co-constructing what they are learning and given choices about applying learning • learning environment encourages research with opportunities to share findings • learning questions used to frame topics and encourage research • all lessons contain opportunities for using and applying skills • children provided with real opportunities to link learning to their world • subject allocation for non-core subjects ensures the arts, PE, PSHE and languages are taught and valued • timetables are flexible for specific pupils when needed • provision is made for specific pupils to extend learning by following interests	
Do we build growth mindset? • uses language of effort, determination and resilience and encourages children to peer-assess learning and model this with class • uses mixed ability groupings and assigns roles to children in leading learning • links rewards to effort • gives written feedback that is specific, helpful and focused on next steps • children are encouraged to value mistakes as new learning • lessons always build in learning time for children to evaluate learning	
Are expectations of the highest standard? • children are shown models of excellent outcomes from beginning of topic (not the end) • expectations posters are visible and referred to in learning by both children and staff • learning environment provides models of excellence for pupils to refer to in every lesson • mid-term planning includes time for redrafting and editing • children are taught collaboration skills to jointly edit, critique and peer-review learning • adults use visualisers/display to celebrate excellent learning • learning topics plan for excellent outcomes in a variety of forms including performance, art, debate, written outcomes	

In three years, pupils from Woodhill were outperforming all pupils nationally, and disadvantaged pupils were twice as likely to reach or exceed national expectations as similar pupils nationally. Relationships drive change.

Key questions to consider:

1 Do all staff model the quality of relationships required for your school to flourish?

2 How does recruitment in your school ensure that you appoint people who value relationships?

3 How does your school celebrate the impact of positive climate and its contribution to whole-school improvement?

4 Are there groups within your school community who do not feel the benefits of a positive culture and climate? If so, what might you do to tackle this?

5 Are you aware of your cultural blind spots? For example, are there aspects of practice that might reinforce negative or positive labels? What might you do about this?

We will now get deeper into the stuff of learning. I will show how learning is as much a social exchange, connected with relationships, motivation and purpose, as it is about knowledge and skills. When learning connects to the 'why', learners are able to see a more expansive horizon for how classroom experiences lead to making a difference. A colleague once reminded me that children did learn to read before instructional phonics schemes were invented – we sometimes need to be reminded about this.

6 The domains of learning

Case study: Chantelle

Chantelle joined as a casual mid-term admission, aged six. She was in Year 1 and had both older and younger siblings who attended the same school, as well as secondary-school-age brothers and sisters, all of whom had been moved around or excluded from many of the local schools. Chantelle was a smaller-than-average child, and was bright, sociable and inquisitive about life. She would notice what you were wearing and how you had your hair and had a heightened sense of awareness of the world around her for someone so young, almost to the point of suspicion; she was sensitive to any change of routine or circumstance in her world.

Within days of joining, it became apparent that Chantelle was a vulnerable child. Her mother was indifferent and apathetic towards her children and was known to social services; her oldest brother had been given a banning order because of violent and anti-social behaviour in the neighbourhood. The first signs of Chantelle's vulnerability were the contrasting behaviours exhibited in the classroom compared to the playground. In play situations, she wanted to be mothered by older pupils and would role-play being a baby while the older pupils fussed over her, plaiting her hair, holding her hand and generally giving her access to their world. Perhaps this softer behaviour was an indication of the love and attention she craved, giving her a much-needed opportunity to become a child again. In the classroom, however, it was a different matter. She was prone to violent rages, which meant the class having to leave the room, which they always did with grace and tolerance. She often refused to engage in learning, would swear loudly and throw objects at the first sign of being challenged by a task or activity. After just a week, the school reported concerns to the allocated social services team, requesting support.

When staff tried to engage mum in discussion, there was a detachment and an unwillingness to engage. Staff began logging concerns about increasingly violent and disruptive actions, especially those associated with classroom learning tasks. Chantelle's outbursts became more disruptive – throwing chairs, hitting staff and pupils, hiding under tables, running out of lessons, swearing repeatedly.

One day, as Chantelle was sketching, she started talking more about her uncle and how she sometimes shared a bed with him at night-time. She also disclosed that she occasionally wet the bed, for which she would be hit. Two days later, Chantelle came to school with a mark on her body. She said she was accidently burned by an iron as her older sibling was preparing the school uniform. Around this point, social services intervened and removed Chantelle from the family home, placing her in temporary foster care.

During the following six months, Chantelle remained in attendance at the school. Throughout this time, she saw her older sister daily at break times, assemblies and lunchtime. The school arranged for times of the day when the girls could play together or even spend time in each other's classrooms. Occasionally she saw her mother bringing the younger child to nursery – on such days, staff would completely alter Chantelle's learning timetable, knowing the disruption that this could cause. The school put in place measures so that she arrived at school via a different entrance. They altered her start time but Chantelle did all she could to subvert these plans. The truth was that Chantelle ached to see her mum and missed her family desperately. If she caught a glimpse of mum – who, by this time, was pregnant again – Chantelle's world fell apart.

The violent behaviour continued and social services spoke about locating Chantelle in a neighbouring authority but were reluctant to do so because they hoped that, with support, Chantelle could be returned to the family home. This plan, however, never came to fruition. More and more was being uncovered about the chaos of Chantelle's first years in life. It transpired that mother was engaged in prostitution and had a history of drug misuse. Other siblings started to speak about the way they had been treated within the home, and the concerns about sexual abuse slowly rose to greater prominence.

Then one terrible day, the police were called to the school because Chantelle's violence had become so disruptive that they could not cope. She had turned a classroom upside down and was a danger to herself as well as others. She threatened staff with scissors, had bitten several staff members and was in emotional crisis. The morning passed, during which time the police remained in school, trying to coax and encourage Chantelle. Staff decided that it would be best to utilise the school counselling service and, as Chantelle had settled, sent the police away. A safe space was found for Chantelle and a dedicated team of staff to remain with her. Slowly, as the day progressed, Chantelle grew calmer and more stable. She began holding conversations again and even picked up a book to read aloud to one of the staff supporting her. They played learning games together and managed the afternoon without further upset.

When home time came and Chantelle's foster carer arrived to take her home, she again exploded. She called the foster carer a 'slag', a 'f*cking bit*h', a 'c*nt' and much more besides. At one point, in the headteacher's office, she threw books, a pencil pot and even a weighted door stop across the room. Social services were called but it was 7.30 pm before Chantelle finally arrived home. When the door to the house of the foster carer was eventually closed, with Chantelle safely inside, staff wept in desperation for her and what her future might bring.

On the following Monday morning, around 7.00 am, the school received a desperate phone call. Chantelle had managed to leave the house and the foster carer did not know where she was. She had dressed herself, taken a bag of belongings and managed to find the keys (which were hung up at adult height in the kitchen), navigate a triple-locked front door, including a heavy-duty mortice lock, and then creep out before anyone else was awake.

Staff and the foster carer were beside themselves. The police were called and a search party of staff were sent out to look for her. The foster carer's house was three miles away from the school and a further half a mile away from Chantelle's family home. They figured out that if she was going to go anywhere, she would head for her mother's house. The problem was that to do so, she would have to cross several busy London roads at commuter time. 9.00 am passed and there was no sign of Chantelle. Her mother hadn't seen her and nor had the police.

Then, at 9.55 am, the school received a call to say that she had been found and was safe. This little six-year-old girl, who had been through so much in her short life, had managed to board a bus and travel several miles, finding herself within the vicinity of the school. She was dressed in school uniform and had her book bag by her side, complete with her parent comments book and a pencil.

The reason for telling this story? Despite everything else that Chantelle had experienced, to this vulnerable and traumatised child, school mattered. There are children with stories like Chantelle in every school. These stories are often untold or remain hidden because we tend not to measure or evaluate a child's wellbeing or capacity for non-cognitive learning in the same way as we do a test score. There are no school benchmarks or performance management targets for children's happiness. It isn't part of a national inspection framework, and too few policymakers understand the social environmental factors that affect our most disadvantaged pupils, or how some schools perform small miracles every day, just to help children like Chantelle feel a tiny bit better. Depressingly, there are also more children like Chantelle in some schools than others. Where there is poverty, poor access to public resources and low social or cultural capital, there will be a Chantelle. The impact of a poor start to life has a dramatic influence on education success, which is a huge factor in life chances.

The key to the success of making Foxfield and Woodhill schools better places to learn was creating a climate where pupils like Chantelle could thrive. To understand how and why we did it, we need to look at the three domains of learning and their place in our current education system.

This chapter will also explore the essential relationship between working and long-term memory and how understanding this can unlock the potential for all pupils to achieve, regardless of circumstance. If there was one element of learning that I wish I had known about when I began teaching, it would be the need for pupils to have more time to engage in practice. It changes everything.

The cognitive learning domain (CLD)

Cognitive learning domain theory builds on the work of Bloom's learning taxonomy (1956). Bloom believed that learning could be organised into the following descriptors and that a hierarchy of status exists between learning levels. Much of what we teach in schools today, including *the way we teach* and our curriculum framework, is organised around this theory:

1 Knowledge: Remembering or retrieving previously learned material.
2 Comprehension: The ability to grasp or construct meaning from material.
3 Application: The ability to use learned material, or to implement material in new and concrete situations.
4 Analysis: The ability to break down or distinguish the parts of material into its components so that its organizational structure may be better understood.
5 Synthesis: The ability to put parts together to form a coherent or unique new whole.
6 Evaluation: The ability to judge, check, and even critique the value of material for a given purpose.

The problem with our obsession with CLD

Although frameworks for a cognitive taxonomy have been revised in different ways, giving greater emphasis to one element or another (SOLO taxonomy being a good example), we prioritise cognitive domain as the standard measure to define learning and use the language associated with cognition to support our evaluation of learning in schools up and down the country. The well-established structure of testing and assessing pupils is also founded on these principles. We test what is easiest to measure, and that tends to be cognitive domain. Test questions, for example, are typically focused on knowledge retrieval, memory recall and application of taught skills, and progressively build towards evaluation and inference. Pupils are taught to value the prize of test scores instead of the precious opportunities afforded to us by making multiple mistakes, learning from error and building expertise gradually over time. Exams are taken in isolation; learning is measured by individual performance. In turn, we treasure the performance of learning more than we do the continuous rehearsals.

To compound the bias, most policymakers, including civil servants, ministers and noted doyens of education, thrived in an environment where success was defined by mastering the high-stakes learning of exam pressures and testing. They look within their own experience to form a narrative about what education should be like for the future, based on their past experience. In this future, learning follows a linear trajectory, defined by predetermined milestones that consist of periodic tests of knowledge, a limited number of skills and their application. Little wonder that organisations such as PwC and the 21C Skills Lab believe we are not preparing pupils to thrive in a complex world. Cognitive domain focus will take us only so far. As Nassim Nicholas Taleb (2018) argues, you can be both intellectual and stupid at the same time.

In traditional models of education (let's call this an 'industrial' model), pupils who fail to grasp the knowledge are given more of the same type of teaching until they are seen to have the core competencies, are placed with younger pupils or are given differentiated tasks that are deemed to be more appropriate for that learner. By contrast, our perceived more-able pupils get to undertake the learning tasks deemed to offer more evaluative opportunities, where they are able to apply knowledge and skills and feed their curiosity for learning.

We have created a kind of education bias, every bit as discriminatory as setting by ability or grouping pupils according to our subjective perceptions of their ability. Our framework for defining learning has, typically, focused on organising classrooms to reflect what is valued through a cognitive lens.

Rarely do we think of learning as non-cognitive, where the 'affective domain' traits, including resilience, motivation and effort, are valued equally to knowledge within the learning process.

Let's imagine another way, using Chantelle as an example. She arrives at school and is immediately assessed using a pupil profile, which helps the school identify her core needs, likes, dislikes, important people to her and ways in which she wants to be supported (see Figure 4, p. 67). From this, a relationship begins to form between staff and Chantelle because we see the child rather than the test score. Chantelle feels valued because, for the first time, she is being asked questions about who she really is, as a person, rather than who she is expected to be.

Alongside this, the school uses a simple rubric that evaluates her essential life skills, including non-cognitive domain qualities. This reveals how Chantelle copes with failure, has the required social skills to collaborate, and her levels of concentration to remain focused on learning tasks. Her teachers identify where her strengths are. She is tenacious but lacks confidence in specific aspects of learning, which leads her to become distracted easily. She is worried about making mistakes and dislikes being seen as a failure. To support her, the teachers work hard to position learning within a framework where making 'useful learning mistakes' is seen as a good thing. She is taught strategies to ask for help and is given language prompts, such as 'the mistake I made was… This helped me to…'

Chantelle is immersed in an environment where all members of the community are learners – where nobody is viewed as 'gifted or talented' but all have equal opportunities to contribute to tasks without the fear of failure. Teachers and staff speak about the value of error-making – they even have displays that show what to do when you do make errors and the strategies to overcome these. Assemblies and other school rituals celebrate learning as a journey rather than an outcome.

Reporting to parents focuses on the broader qualities of being a twenty-first-century learner. Workshops are held so that parents understand that cognitive domain versus non-cognitive domain learning is not a binary world view but is intrinsically linked to life success in an increasingly complex world. For the first time, Chantelle begins to understand that she isn't defined by being clever but more by her ability to demonstrate the resilience to overcome the barriers that have defined her classroom experiences. She starts to feel proud when she doesn't give up on a learning task or when she is able to reframe a mistake as a new opportunity. She even begins to show her teacher examples of her own learning mistakes when she has made them.

Our reliance on CLD is a fundamental issue with our system and has had a damaging impact on our most disadvantaged pupils, especially in regions where there are big discrepancies in social mobility. For our most persistently disadvantaged, some of whom enter formal education without their learning toolkit topped up, the achievement gaps between them and other pupil groups are stubbornly resistant to closure. In 2016, the percentage of those pupils most affected by disadvantage achieving the expected standard of English and maths was just 39 per cent, compared to 60 per cent of non-disadvantaged pupils (DfE, 2016). We also know that the perception of the teacher in grouping pupils plays a big role in how confident pupils feel about learning. Pupils as young as six or seven are extremely conscious of their ranking in the classroom compared to other pupils. According to Jo Boaler (2005), from Stanford University, 88 per cent of pupils placed in sets aged four remained in those groupings until they leave school. Perceptions matter.

As Sir John Jones famously quoted: 'Whether you think a child can, or whether you think they cannot, you will be right.' (Jones, 2009) Self-efficacy and belief matter. Our education system is afflicted by limiting beliefs about pupils that have nothing to do with their potential for success, but everything to do with the labels we have become accustomed to using. Phrases like 'gifted', 'high flyer' and 'natural talent' support the myth that failure in education has nothing to do with teaching and everything to do with innate ability. Typically, we associate these traits with cognitive learning domain instead of our capacity to grow as learners.

Labels can be self-imposed by the learner or ingrained within school culture. They can be hard to shift and can have a debilitating impact on children's achievement. Positive labels carry a badge that creates fixed-mindset thinking – creating fear of losing status. Negative labels can be self-fulfilling. Labels also create hierarchy and social status. We can be excluded from or gain entry to education acceptability simply because of perception.

Internationally too, with the advancement of capitalism and globalisation, it has been accepted that cognitive learning is the dominant measure of what learning is. With the acceptance of PISA comparisons, teachers have faced more and more pressure to increase achievement scores in reading and maths. Governments, internationally, have based most, if not all, policy reform around cognitive domain.

And just as we have sought to implement policy reform based on cognition (the drive to produce pupils as clever as those in South East Asia), so has teacher evaluation and assessment reform followed suit. The new national curriculum and changes to assessment, introduced in 2015 ignored everything we know about how learning really happens at a deep level: namely that through interaction with other people and connection with the world – in other words, through relationships. This has led the profession down a dangerous path where we evaluate the quality of the *teacher*, rather than the *teaching*. And the measures for evaluating the teacher have been simplistic and based mainly on outcomes for pupils: those teachers who help pupils attain the highest grades are perceived to be more valuable than those who don't. The argument has followed that if we remove from our schools the lowest quality teachers, then the overall quality of the teaching will increase.

The problem with this model is that, perhaps, the best-perceived teachers might also be subject to the same kinds of bias that disadvantaged children face. In schools that value the wrong kind of learning and the wrong teaching strategies, what might be perceived as 'good teaching' could otherwise be described as 'training' children to pass tests.

The affective learning domain (ALD)

Affective domain is more complex and nuanced to the context of learning:

1 Receiving: Awareness of the world and wider environment.

2 Responding: Motivation and willingness to learn.

3 Valuing: Beliefs and attitudes, commitment to learning and an acceptance that the learning has a value.

4 Organisation: Internalisation of the learning in order to construct new or wider meaning related to the learning.

5 Characterisation: The internalisation of values or wider beliefs where the learning impacts on broader attitudes about life.

Like cognitive domain, affective domain can also be divided into a hierarchy, but it is more concerned with feelings, motives or emotions. Essentially, affective domain is concerned with the relationship between learner and learning concept. Affective domain connects much more deeply with the 'why' of learning so that, within the higher order of the taxonomy, learners form a lasting bond with the learning content. Simon Sinek (2011, p.39) explains:

> 'Very few people or companies clearly articulate WHY they do WHAT they do. By WHY I mean what is your purpose, cause or belief? The most successful leaders and organisations do not invest all of their energies on the "what" or "how" of their work. Instead, they focus on the why. Starting with why shifts leadership away from getting people to do things, to feeling deeply connected to the moral purpose and core values. People don't follow you because of what or how, they do it because of "why".'

Table 8 There are many reasons why we should start with 'why'

Why? (Purpose and cause)	How? (Actions)	What? (Impact)
Provides moral purpose for change.	Inspires/connects vision with cause.	Creates teams. Galvanises 'followers' of the cause.
Specifies long-term goals (aspirational).	Specifies methods (transformational).	Creates discretionary effort (long-term investment in shared success).
Passionate and compassionate leadership.	Releases talent and loosens control.	Solves complex problems through common ownership.
Nurtures curiosity, understanding and observation and…	…deepens questioning which leads to…	…change and action.
Values-based but needs…	…authentic leadership…	…to create trust and empowerment.
Sustainable leadership is not built on *what* you do or *how* you do it, it is framed around *why*. Starting with *why* shifts the leadership paradigm away from getting people to do thinks (command, compliance and control) to shared thinking and ownership of change. It enables you to co-design and construct the future you want from the beginning.		

The merits of ALD

One could argue that affective domain is a prerequisite for cognitive learning to take place. If you are not committed to the learning content, how else can you use it to make a difference beyond the school? The better we connect learning to moral purpose, the deeper the relationship between the learning and learner. This takes us back to the 'why' question.

However, we rarely speak about the importance of affective domain. Why not? It does not form part of our curriculum framework, it is not something we regularly assess for, at least beyond the Early Years curriculum, and it is not spoken about by politicians or policymakers as the real currency for our economic success. Nobody says, 'we need to teach our children how to be more globally in tune with the economic disadvantages of Brexit'. I have never heard an inspector commenting on the depth of internalisation of a learning concept to help a pupil make sense of the learning in school within the wider world.

The answers to why we do not give affective domain more explicit prominence within our curriculum are twofold. Firstly, affective domain learning is harder to assess than cognitive domain. It requires one to take a broader and longer view of curriculum provision and assessment. You can't just *teach* affective domain thinking and then write a test paper to evaluate pupils' learning. It is the underpinning of a whole belief system and is deeply connected to a values base. It is about growing – what Bob Chapman describes as 'conscious leadership'. Affective domain is closely linked to the culture and climate within a school. It necessitates a framework for teaching that goes beyond surface-level reproducing learning or teaching children to pass tests. It is fundamentally about deep learning. ALD necessitates that children fail and learn; it means promotion of risk-taking, confidence-building, growth mindset and our ability to challenge perceptions in an appropriate way. It takes a brave headteacher, committed to building a learning philosophy around the affective domain, simply because the results, while much greater and more potent, are not a quick-fix solution. You can't build affective domain through booster classes. It is a little bit like the football manager who buys players for today and ignores the future by failing to develop the talent of the young players in the football squad.

Let's take the example of learning in Photo 11, p. 80, to illustrate my point. Howard is a Year 2 pupil who writes a fantastic account about how aluminium cans are recycled. Ask him to produce a 'hot write' or a 'cold write' – I'm a fan of neither – and we get little emotional response. However, take Howard (as we did) to the aluminium can recycling plant, tell him that we are going to produce pamphlets to campaign for the need to recycle more, explain to Howard's family that we want to assess the impact of Howard's learning about recycling aluminium cans on his wider attitude to global awareness, and we get a very different response. The trigger for Howard to write so enthusiastically has as much to do with his motivation to want to write for a real cause as it does his knowledge of phonemes and graphemes. This is an example of affective domain.

The second reason we have not prioritised affective learning domain is more political. I grew up in a single-parent household on a council estate in Swindon. I attended my local primary school and then a comprehensive secondary school, which had a broad intake of pupils from the local area. My exposure to the richness of language, the nuance of argument or the different ways in which points of view could be interpreted was limited by the direct impact of my experiences and the social exchanges between family members or at school. I did not grow up in a household rich in what Robin Alexander (2017) would describe as 'dialogic talk'. By this, I refer to how interaction with others and with language constructs helped me to create a schema of thinking for meaning, allowing me to build learning capital beyond the cognitive domain.

In fact, it was not until I went on a school trip to the House of Commons at around 12 years old that it hit me square in the face: the sharp contrast between *my* world view of how things were and the opportunities provided to those with greater social and cultural capital. I am not for one second suggesting that affective domain potential is limited by social or financial status. I am arguing that there are higher levels of capital, including language development and a broader set of experiences, that help young people make greater sense of the world around them that come from privilege. For example, much of the criticism aimed at the 2016 Key Stage 2 reading test came from the view that the

> 10.2.11
>
> Each ingot can create 1.5 million cans!
> Next a big roller squezes the ingot. As a result
> the ingot becomes thinner and longer.
> Even when its squezesed its still strong
> because it has lots of rigity and (it is) light
> wiegt. Fren chaly they make sheets of
> alumilim that are 18 km! Each alumilim
> sheet is ensured (checked to) so the sheet is the right
> thickness. Then they get loaded on to a
> truck and prepare to be transported to
> the can making plant.

Photo 11 *Howard's writing demonstrates an example of affective domain*

language was harder for disadvantaged pupils to access because it did not translate to their experiences as learners – affective domain. In other words, as Robin Alexander (2017, p.18) writes in *Towards Dialogic Teaching*:

> *'Political prejudice and the inherited educational culture have continued to frustrate the breakthrough which is needed. What adds urgency to this agenda is that children's access to opportunities for talk outside school vary considerably, as do the quality and potency of the talk they encounter.'*

Unfortunately, policymakers largely fail to understand this. Education policies have been developed on the premise that all pupils have equal access to the same social and cultural tools because those who create policy are surrounded by similar people who have had a similar experience and think similar things. They think that the main skill is for pupils to pass exams written by people like them, or to write papers to be read by people like them. Their mental construct of education replicates their own world view about how schools should be because they are blind to the challenges faced by pupils not from their backgrounds. The latest fad for the knowledge-based curriculum, facts and information is a good example of how this translates into education folklore. Suddenly, the reason why our schools are not successful is because we are not all teaching pupils the Latin derivations of commonly misspelt words.

The psychomotor learning domain (PLD)

The third domain of learning is psychomotor domain. Put simply, the psychomotor domain concerns the specific-to-discrete physical functions, including reflex actions and interpretive movements. This includes the physical encoding of information with movement and/or activities where the gross and fine muscles are used for expressing or interpreting information or concepts. A good example of this would be how the physical process of handwriting can support one's ability to remember spellings.

As a hierarchy, the psychomotor domain is broken into the following areas:

1   Reflex movement: Natural reflex of limbs as we involuntarily move or develop as infants.

2   Fundamental movement: Components for more complex actions like walking, running or jumping.

3   Perceptual abilities: Skills related to kinaesthetic (bodily movements), visual, auditory, tactile (touch) or coordination abilities.

4   Physical abilities: Related to endurance, flexibility, agility, strength, reaction–response time or dexterity.

5   Skilled movements: Skills and movements that must be learned for games, sports, dances, performances or the arts.

6   Non-discursive communication: Expressive movements through posture, gestures, facial expressions and/or creative movements like those in mime or ballet. These movements refer to interpretative movements that communicate meaning without the aid of verbal commands or help.

(Adapted from Floyd, 2016)

Education theory connecting the psychomotor domain with other domains of learning has centred on the concept of deliberate practice and the mythical 10,000 hours required to transmit learning from working memory to long-term memory. The argument follows that the 10,000 hours rule holds the secret to success for learning in any field, as long it's the right practice. This is where psychomotor domain and other learning domains merge in significance. We don't increase learning simply by physical and mental repetition but through continual adjustment of our physical actions with the mindset to be successful. What we need to encourage is smart practice, not any practice.

Psychomotor domain is therefore intrinsically linked to affective domain in that to maintain a focus on smart practice, we need to maintain a positive lens on what we do in the practice zone. The best coaching for positive practice focuses on what pupils can do rather than what they cannot. It holds the ratio of praise in favour of encouragement to at least 2:9 and moves the conversations about improvement gradually to extract concrete goals from a vision of where we might get to – with support. This is why (according to Daniel Coyle (2010) and other psychologists, including Daniel Goleman (2013)) the best coaches are those who have often failed in an aspect of excellence they coach in (or have learned to bounce back from failure) and who have the attention to detail to ensure that any practice of learning enables practice to move into perfect over time.

The second important point to make about psychomotor domain is its connection with long-term memory. We will examine this more closely in Chapter 7, but it is relevant to note now that we are most likely to free up working memory slots, thus freeing our long-term memory to deliver the capacity we need it to, when we enjoy our learning. When we love what we do (affective domain), it leads to a high-absorption, all-consuming emotional flow, where time becomes meaningless as we engage in what switches us on. If we channel these moments well, we have the capacity to enhance learning potential inexorably. The problem is, according to Daniel Goleman (2013), that only about 20 per cent of us feel these moments on a daily basis. As we connect the domains of learning together and value their significance as intrinsically linked, we begin to see the importance of a broader curriculum and more expansive framework to define learning – one that moves beyond basic knowledge and skills.

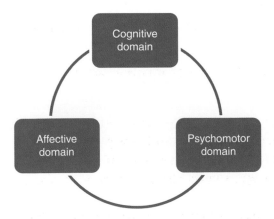

Figure 5 *Great teaching continuously weaves between the domains of learning*

An alternative approach

Great schools often subvert government policy or use it to their advantage. They fight for more autonomy and value a bespoke approach to learning, based on a compelling need to ensure that the learning deepens the quality of the learning experience, helping pupils make a bigger connection with the wider world.

Rather than basing learning solely around the cognitive domain, our most effective schools radiate core learning competencies (non-cognitive domains), leading to pupils developing citizenship, social entrepreneurism, creativity and deeper connections between learning and moral purpose.

Unfortunately, these qualities are not reflected in high-stakes and high-profile PISA test score headlines or, at a national level, in Ofsted reports and exam results. The problem in our quest to understand how to raise standards in the UK has been the fact that we are unable to recognise that learning takes many forms, is complex and cannot be evaluated through a cognitive learning lens alone. If ideas are the new currency of learning and a more 'organic' approach to learning is needed, we need to let go of the industrial model.

Peter Block's book *Community: The Structure of Belonging* (2008) offers an alternative vision to the industrial one, providing a model for learning and leadership in the twenty-first century that is better matched to the complex nature of learning, working for the good of all. He argues that invested learning communities necessitate interdependence and that growth occurs when everyone sees themselves as investors, owners and creators of change.

To achieve this, schools have to create a values-led approach to the organisation of learning in schools. This includes:

1 Recognising that learning communities are created when we concentrate on people's gifts rather than deficiencies.

2 Engaging all community members in the process of a common vision for learning.

3 Understanding that success depends on everybody achieving (rather than the few) and that success is driven by relationships.

4 Recognising that sustained improvement is achieved only when learning communities are given the power and permission to act.

5 Understanding that lasting success is gained not through economic achievement but by harnessing social capital.

Ownership and belonging come from and lead to deeper levels of conversation and mutual investment in a school's values and beliefs. Leadership of learning is demonstrated not by mandating change but by creating a climate where change flourishes. 'What makes community building so complex is that it occurs in an infinite number of small steps.' (Block, 2008, p. 9)

Comparisons between schools and the medical profession highlight the complexity of leadership in organisations where relationships within a community define success or

Table 9 A variety of learning models for the twenty-first century can be defined (adapted from Robinson and Aronica, 2015)

	The industrial model	The organic model	Professional practice
Ways of thinking	Traditional learning. A 'training' approach to teaching and learning. Good for focusing on 'how to' and 'what' of learning.	Engaging Learning. A personalised approach to teaching and learning. Focuses on the 'why' of learning.	Expansive. Provides the moral purpose which connects the 'why' of learning with the 'how' and 'what' through school values and building learning dispositions.
Purpose	Provides specific knowledge and skills linked to a set context or framework. Builds knowledge/skills sequentially in linear fashion.	Connects interdisciplinary learning skills and critical thinking. Provides a bridge between knowledge and skills with purpose, meaning and evaluation of learning. Provides space for reflection and continuous improvement.	Defines boundaries of possibility. Provides a bridge between community, formal education and understanding within the wider world. Helps develop life and career skills. Builds leaning characteristics.
Characteristics	Instructional. Rigid. Outcomes focused. linked to specific knowledge sets and pre-defined curriculum content. Scheme driven. Builds procedural fluency within boundaries of learning context.	Enquiry driven, linked to multiple contexts and pupil interests. Develops learning from conceptual understanding to extended abstract. Builds expansive language and meaning through dialogic talk.	Interdisciplinary. Blends academic and vocational disciplines. Provides expansive programmes for organisation of learning based on framework of skills and knowledge to be understood. Does not discriminate between value of subjects and disciplines.
Organisation	Predominantly adult led. Whole class/groups. Multiple opportunities for practising. Builds skills through repetition and acquisition of knowledge/skills. Assessment mainly summative.	Adult and peer led. Organic and open ended. Multiple opportunities for collaboration and evaluation of learning. Builds communication, language and critical thinking. Assessment is formative, summative and ipsative.	School/community/culturally driven. Defines the culture and climate within school. Led by values and what matters most. Holistic. Cross-cultural and cross-curricular. Establishes learning community.

	The industrial model	The organic model	Professional practice
Values	Looking backwards historically, rote learning, testing, procedure, sequencing, instruction, how to, what to, standardisation.	Looking forwards, relational learning, theory of learning, complexity, co-construction and design, personalisation, innovation, individual talents, creativity.	Research and evidence to inform policy, relationships, inclusion, individual and collective successes across spectrum of learning disciplines.
Best for…	Routine and establishing rules for learning. Builds confidence within parameters of context for learning. Prepares pupils for exam success. Good for setting direction and focus of learning. Can build learning stamina within set discipline.	Enabling diversity of skills to shine across disciplines. Critical thinking, problem solving and application of learning. Gives equal balance between skills for education, life and application in real world. Promotes leadership and social responsibility giving purpose to learning.	Establishing whole-school climate for learning. Developing collective values. Learning habits which span economic, social and cultural development. Celebrating individual and collective talents and skills across leaning disciplines. Leadership.

failure. Process-management systems should not replace professional judgement and are often over-focused on deficiencies rather than assets (e.g. people). By contrast, the investment in relationships across a community enhances the social capital of the whole, rather than the individual, and also creates a cause for improvement. It is this discretionary effort that underpins the fabric of a learning community and dictates the pace and tone of improvement within a school.

Peter Block's *Community* offers a number of insights and a historical perspective about how leadership can impact on building 'community' within our schools. He describes the paradox in how the shrinking effect of globalisation is actually creating more fragmented, disconnected and marginalised communities, and how gaps are widening between the haves and have nots. Chasing grades and target-setting has had a negative impact on society and the wellbeing of the communities we serve. We have lost sight of what is really important, including our need to help create a better world. A good education system in a bad world does not seem right, fair or just. Perhaps, if we can learn to value the non-cognitive domain learning traits, we have an opportunity to change that.

So how do we ensure that pupils like Chantelle receive the very best education experiences? Given the widening gaps between our most advantaged and disadvantaged pupils, not just here in the UK but also internationally, how do we address the imbalance of education and also the imbalance of opportunity to ensure that for our most challenged pupils, as Robin Alexander (2017) argues, 'the talk [for learning] that they engage in at school is nothing less than a lifeline'? To answer this question, I want us to go back to Woodhill Primary School in South East London.

An expansive curriculum

After the damning 2013 Ofsted report, Woodhill had (by 2017) posted three years of successive assessment results that were above national statistics at every key stage. The percentage of pupils working at 'greater depth' learning was more than double that of the national average from 2016. The overall percentage of pupils at Key Stage 2 achieving the expected standard in reading, writing and maths was 21 per cent higher than the national standard. In all aspects, the school is a success story – the kind of story that needs to be told. It demonstrates that there are no glass ceilings to what can be achieved, for even our most disadvantaged pupils, when the climate and conditions for excellence are owned by the whole community. But what is the undistorted truth about the school's progress journey versus the perceived?

Consistency and higher expectations

Viewed through the lens of accountability, we could argue that the school embarked on a journey to instil consistency and higher expectations across key stages. We could say that leaders focused on non-negotiable core standards and made concerted efforts to deliver instructional change, which resulted in higher achievement grades for pupils. This would provide a strategic narrative, no doubt impressing some people.

At Woodhill, the mindset shift was as much about the individual parents who supported the school by attending learning coffee mornings, and the NQTs who worked so hard to collaborate with teachers between schools so that they could perfect and polish their craft of teaching as it was about any leadership team. The real truth of the success is that affective domain learning matters at least as much as cognitive domain learning.

A holistic learning profile

All pupils who attend Woodhill receive a holistic profile, which captures their learning needs and interests. The profile goes beyond cognitive domain and captures their aspirations, hopes and dreams. These are used to support planning for learning which follows pupils' interests and provides a global perspective on the world.

They help to make learning more meaningful and personalised to the needs of each child. The school has created a nurture provision to wrap around our most vulnerable pupils when they are in crisis. There is an experienced inclusion team with specialist qualifications in behaviour leadership, autism training and social care. This team meets regularly to evaluate, review and map provision in a connected way. Teachers, parents and children are involved in the process so that the pupil voice is heard at every stage. And the team also includes Benji, the school dog. Benji attends school daily and is a part of the lives of children. He hears children read, has a structured timetable to help pupils build confidence and has been as important as any staff member in helping create a community that values learning.

The core curriculum provision is broad, ambitious and expansive. It teaches children how to live as well as how to learn. It includes planned and structured mindfulness lessons that teach pupils how to reflect. In 2016–17, the school spent more of its CPD budget on emotional wellbeing training than any other curriculum area.

By 2017, Woodhill had appointed specialist teachers for computing, art and PE. But these teachers do not just teach the subjects, they co-construct by planning with other teachers, modelling lessons and leading coaching support so that teachers gain the valuable experience of learning alongside experts.

Positive approaches to 'mistakes'

The school has developed learning postcards to support teachers, children and parents in being able to respond to 'useful learning mistakes'. The postcards help to ensure that lessons in school and learning beyond give pupils the necessary tools to persuade, influence, reason and reflect. If the children do not arrive at school with the same experiences and cultural capital as those who are more privileged, staff insist that it is their duty to provide the lifeline. And it works. In 2016, the school widened its use of learning postcards (see Photo 12) to parents and families. Parents were trained to use the language of learning reflection at home to reinforce the messages at school. The postcards included scaffolds and prompts such as:

1   What did you learn in school from a friend that will help you tomorrow?

2   Find an example of learning that you can use at home.

3   Can you describe a specific moment in a lesson that helped you the most? Why was this?

Widening pupils' prospects

In addition, the school developed a learning charter (Photo 13) that captures the core learning experiences we believe are the entitlement of every child who attends the school. The school development plan includes a five-year strategy to deepen pupil voice and pupil leadership across our school community so that our pupils, who gaze out towards the River Thames and the Canary Wharf complex from their flats, can dream that one day they will be in positions to deliver on our collective promise to create a better world than the one we have today.

Learning dispositions

The school also developed a framework for evaluating learning dispositions, which is every bit as important as an accountability framework that measures only cognitive domain learning.

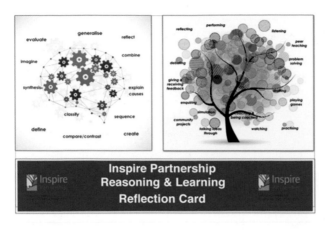

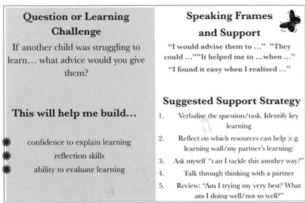

Photo 12 *Reasoning and learning reflection cards were used at home to reinforce the school messages*

The learning dispositions continuum supports pupils in building metacognition and staff in their understanding of how non-cognitive domain traits lead to improved life chances.

The continuum helps pupils to take greater ownership of their learning and that of others. It also provides a scaffold for teachers to deepen thinking about how pupils learn best and how we assess more than subject-specific skills and knowledge.

Similarly, staff devised a framework to help teachers understand the learning skills we value most so that practitioners avoid teaching narrow, disconnected units of learning that focus only on cognitive domain.

One of our biggest tasks as teachers and leaders in schools is to grasp the ethical and moral implications of our actions, decisions and behaviours. These influence beliefs and values. We have created schools whose sole focus is to ensure that pupils achieve high grades and meet the expectations of predefined standards. Despite our 'why' being absolutely critical to the success of our children, we have lost sight of it. Too many within our communities feel unheard, under-represented and disconnected from decision-making processes. A thriving education system in a world of disadvantage, inequality and poor equity is an unacceptable paradox.

WOODHILL PRIMARY SCHOOL

LEARNING

CHARTER

AT WOODHILL WE ASPIRE FOR ALL CHILDREN TO BE:

- Confident learners who are motivated, independent and curious about the world
- Learners with the skills to enter employment and make a difference
- Ambitious for both themselves and the contributions they make to society

OUR CORE LEARNING PRINCIPLES

- We are lifelong learners and always learning
- **Diversity is celebrated and used to provide unique learning experiences**
- Parents and families are partners in education
- **Quality learning happens when learners are stimulated and challenged**
- Learning experiences connect with real life and problem solving
- **Exciting and varied opportunities for educational visits enhance our learning**
- High expectations for all children ensures everyone makes good progress and achieves their best
- **We learn best by learning together and through collaboration**
- Learning is personalised to individuals' needs
- **Learners develop the skills, knowledge and understanding to be confident users of technology**

WOODHILL IS THE PLACE TO LEARN!

- Outstanding learning environments and the highest expectations
- Ambitious curriculum, which links learning to the real world, sports, the arts and problem solving
- Situated on the River Thames, incorporating a world heritage site, museums and rich cultural diversity

"I REALLY ENJOY LEARNING AT WOODHILL PRIMARY SCHOOL. THE LESSONS ARE FUN AND CHALLENGING. WE GET TO GO ON LOTS OF TRIPS AND THE TEACHERS HELP US GET BETTER WITH OUR LEARNING."
YEAR 6 PUPIL

WOODHILL
PRIMARY SCHOOL

Photo 13 *The Woodhill Learning Charter captures the core learning experiences that every child who attends the school is entitled to*

Table 10 The learning dispositions continuum provides a scaffold for teachers and helps pupils take greater ownership of their learning

	Definition	Emerging	Developing	Highly accomplished	Embedded excellence
Questions	A way of finding out	I don't ask too many questions	I can answer 'shallow' questions	I use a wider range of questions – 'shallow' and 'deep' – to find information	I constantly ask questions to seek further information and deepen my understanding
Reflection	Thinking about and looking back on the learning to decide how it went and where to go next	I am not sure what reflection is and what it means but I do want to learn more about this	I am reflecting on my learning with support or prompts – e.g. question starters or feedback marking	I know reflection is an important part of the learning process. I can talk about when, what and how I reflect	I understand reflection helps me with my learning. I use it continuously across a range of situations
Thinking	Reasoning about, reflecting or pondering	I don't usually think much during the learning and do not make connections between areas of learning	With support I can use thinking organisers and strategies to further my learning	I can use various thinking tools and strategies to deepen my thinking and learning	I naturally select the most appropriate thinking tool and strategy to reach a decision, outcome, solution or situation I am faced with
Connections	Linking knowledge together to create new understanding	I find it hard to make connections or links but I am ready to learn about this	I can sometimes make connections, often with support or modelling. Sometimes I have an 'ah ha' moment and I see a link or connection	I make many links and connections between pieces of knowledge to create new ideas or deepen understanding	I constantly look for and use knowledge to connect with old and new learning to develop new understanding. I can talk about this and share with others

Determination	*The ability to stick at a challenge task when you feel like giving up. The desire and determination to self-improve and succeed*	If things are too tricky I often give up. Sometimes I don't and I want to have more determination	I can self-talk to show determination with tasks that are a little more tricky and I can self-motivate to keep going	I have a number of strategies that help me to be determined when tasks are challenging. I can give examples of these	I am determined to self-improve to achieve my very best. I choose from a range of strategies to overcome obstacles and problem-solve. I identify and commit to achieving the next learning steps
Self-awareness	*Aware of yourself as a learner – your actions, thoughts, strengths and next steps*	I am not sure of the things that might help me to become a better learner but I do want to know more about this	I am beginning to build awareness of what I need to do to become a better learner. I can identify some next steps to improve	I am self-aware in my actions and reflection to improve and develop my strengths. I independently work towards achieving my next steps	I am conscious of what makes me 'tick' (strengths, next steps, thoughts and personality traits). I am self-motivated and self-aware of actions I need to improve as a learner
Wonder	*To be amazed at something; the desire to know something*	I am not sure what it means to 'wonder' but there are some things I am really interested in	I sometimes wonder and imagine	I can wonder about ideas and imagine possibilities from one or two perspectives	I wonder to come up with ideas about what 'might be' from many different perspectives. I can elaborate on these ideas and come up with ideas. I can distinguish between wonderings I can act on and wonderings that are unobtainable

Table 11 A framework for personal learning and thinking skills helps teachers understand those skills we value most (adapted from Qualifications and Curriculum Authority, 2007)

	Focus	Is embedded when children:
Independent learners	Children process and evaluation information to work out what they have to do in order to be successful. They take and use information to make reasoned decisions. they recognise that others may have different opinions and different ways of being successful.	• identify questions and problem solve. • plan and conduct research. • explore issues, events or problems from different perspectives. • analyse and evaluate information, measuring its value and relevance. • consider the impact of circumstance, beliefs and feelings on decisions. • support conclusions using evidence and reasoning.
Creative learners	Children think creatively by generating and exploring ideas, making original connections. They try different ways to tackle a problem, working with others to find imaginative, valuable solutions and outcomes.	• generate ideas and explore possibilities. • ask questions to extend thinking. • connect their own and other's ideas and experiences in creative ways. • question their own and others' presumptions about ideas and thinking. • try out new solutions and follow ideas through. • adapt ideas as circumstances change.
Reflective learners	Children evaluate their strengths and limitations, setting themselves realistic goals with criteria for success. They monitor their own performance and process, inviting feedback from others and making changes to further their own learning.	• asses themselves and others, identifying opportunities and achievements. • set goals with success criteria for their development and learning improvements. • review their progress, responding to feedback and making improvements. • invite feedback and deal positively with praise, setbacks and criticism. • evaluate learning experiences and use these to help with new learning. • communicate learning in different ways including with different audiences.
Team learners	Children learn confidently with others, adapting to different contexts and taking responsibility for their own learning. They listen to and take account of different viewpoints. They form collaborative relationships and can resolve issues to be successful.	• collaborate with others when learning for common goals and outcomes. • reach agreements, managing discussions to achieve results. • adapt behaviour in different situations and roles, including leadership roles. • show fairness and consideration to others. • take responsibility, showing confidence in themselves and their contribution to learning. • provide kind, helpful and constructive feedback to others.

	Focus	Is embedded when children:
Self-learners	Children organise themselves, showing personal responsibility, initiative, creativity and enterprise with a commitment to learning and improving learning. They actively embrace change, responding positively to new situations. They look for new opportunities and cope well with change.	• seek out challenges or new responsibilities. • show flexibility when things change. • work towards goals, showing commitment and perseverance. • organise themselves well, including completing tasks within agreed timescales. • deal with pressure and the demands of a busy classroom. • manage emotions well and build positive relationships.
Effective learners	Children actively engage with learning and the life of the school. They play a full role within the school and wider community by taking on responsibilities for improvements for others and themselves.	• discuss learning or issues of concern and seek resolutions where appropriate. • present a persuasive case for actions based on evidence or reasons. • propose practical ways forward, breaking these down into manageable steps. • identify improvements that benefit others as well as themselves. • try to influence other positively by negotiating differences of opinion. • act as an advocate for other children whose opinions might be different from their own.

Learning for the future

It is my feeling that what we value in learning and how our schools learn to be more connected in a world that is changing rapidly. I want to share the perspective of CEOs (chief executive officers) who took part in the PwC Global CEO Report 2017, an annual survey of CEO attitudes towards the future of business and leadership, to demonstrate the importance of the affective learning domain.

PwC has published an annual report, capturing the hopes and fears of international CEOs, every year for the past 20 years. During this time, CEOs have witnessed tremendous upheavals, as a result of globalisation and technological change. Tracking back through the reports, which share the thoughts of nearly 1,400 CEOs, provides both insight and perspective about our socio-economic present and our future. The 2016 CEO report, for example, highlighted that CEOs were extremely concerned about geo-political uncertainty that exists in our world. Six months after the report was published, the UK voted to leave the European Union, and 11 months after, Donald Trump was unexpectedly elected president of the United States. In 2016, the report also stated that 72 per cent of CEOs were worried about the lack of key skills in their organisations at a time when around 48 per cent of those spoken to were planning on increasing their workforces. The 2016 report commented that 75 per cent of CEOs believed that a skilled, educated and adaptable workforce should be a priority for business. But what types of skills were CEOs referring to – cognitive domain or affective domain? The report specifically highlighted a growing concern over the lack of these skills in our young people: teamwork; creativity; problem-solving; adaptability; people skills; and relationship skills.

Brian Moynihan, quoted in the 2016 CEO report, said, 'Even with all the new technology, people skills are actually more important now. Whether it's providing day to day services in our bank branches or managing in our data analytics: it's all about people.'

PwC have embraced this challenge and have developed the concept of the 'PwC Professional'. They have listed the qualities they look for in all employees, and developed professional development programmes to build these skills across the organisation. The PwC Professional is one who is expected to demonstrate:

- relationships
- business acumen
- technical capabilities
- global acumen.

These are broad skills that push way beyond cognitive domain. When we examine them even closer, these include:

- core values
- trust
- collaboration
- authenticity
- resilience
- inclusivity
- passion.

This could almost be a description of the characteristics of effective learners that we define for pupils in the Early Years!

The 2017 20th PwC CEO report goes even further. Referring to the seismic changes in the world over the past 20 years, Bob Moritz reflects that building trust in leadership at times of heightened global anxiety in a world with jagged edges is of paramount importance. He alludes to the lack of faith in our political system and in companies to lead with a defining sense of moral purpose. He also makes an explicit point about our need to root action and behaviours in the 'why':

'The contemporary worker is keenly aware of the importance of purpose – and is demanding clarity on not just the "how" of the company, but the "why." Enduring winners will be leaders who develop a two-way relationship – whether with customers, employees, or society at large – based on reliability and ethical behaviour.'

Key questions to consider:

1 How do teachers plan to incorporate awareness of learning domains in their daily teaching sequences and planning for learning?

2 Are there strengths and gaps in aspects of staff knowledge and understanding of the different learning domains?

3 What elements within the learning domains does your school value more or less? Are there any related actions to take because of this?

4 How well do pupils understand the different learning domains and their impact on how we feel as learners?

5 How well do we evaluate learning successes across the domains of learning? Is there more we can do and, if so, what?

In the next chapter, we will consider mastery for learning, which begins with us and our need to see the purpose of education as one that deepens moral and ethical responsibility. When learning connects with a reason or cause, it strengthens the relationship between learning skills and learning attitudes (affective domain). Viewed this way, mastery of learning is less a checklist of skills performed and more a whole-school approach to the organisation of curriculum, which builds on knowledge but requires application, reasoning and evaluation – in other words, helping pupils move from shallow to deep learning.

7 Mastery for learning

The principle of mastery, as adapted by the great Renaissance artists of Florence, is that we move through a process of learning competency, from novice to expert, over an extended period of time, acquiring skills and deepening our learning incrementally. The model necessitates that learners are taught conceptual understanding alongside practical opportunities to practise and apply new skills with varying degrees of challenge. In other words, we grow from apprentice to master gradually, making incremental gains and learning from mistakes along the way. The mastery approach is a learning framework in which the learner moves from fidelity to being able to apply procedural fluency, as taught or instructed by the teacher. Expertise comes from the confidence to experiment, apply learning in new contexts or play creatively with learning elements – to focus so deeply that we can see the whole picture of learning with complete clarity.

Daniel Coyle (2010) argues that deliberate practice, alongside struggle, leads to myelin, a neural insulator, wrapping itself around the neurons when learning takes place. The thicker the myelin wraps itself around, the better it insulates and the more permanent the learning becomes. The trick is to ensure that the right learning is taking place, with the correct levels of instruction, alongside opportunities to practise as well as learn from failure. When it comes from learning, we become clever through our mistakes. It is by accepting this concept that we begin to see why cognitive learning domain has to sit alongside affective domain.

Mastery in schools

The mastery teaching sequence, as we know it from a school context, has been adapted from these principles so that it knits within a learning paradigm that is fit for purpose in classrooms. It is a pragmatic approach in that it is also a structural tool to support whole-class teaching and embodies other pedagogical principles, including collaboration, feedback and differentiation. By contrast, a 'classic' model of learning is based on all pupils being given the same amount of time to learn content but given different tasks depending on their perceived ability. This was widely viewed to be the preferred model for teaching English and maths during the 1990s, when the numeracy and literacy hour lessons were conceived. The teaching focus was firmly on allocated time for tasks, where pupils were given different tasks to complete based on perceived ability, often without formal teacher instruction to scaffold their learning development. It was crude and based on no sound concept of pedagogy.

By contrast, the mastery model was developed by Benjamin Bloom, who investigated the most effective components of tutoring and adapted them for whole-class teaching. The model consists of:

- dividing up concepts into smaller units
- implementing frequent assessments
- followed by instructor feedback and direction on how to improve
- revisiting key concepts to ensure mastery.

The other element of a mastery teaching model, which is to be welcomed, is that it builds on our understanding of how pupils learn concepts that are *concrete* before those that are *abstract*. Many of the published schemes of work that have emerged in the past three years have provided useful resources that help pupils build strong mental models based on concrete experiences and manipulation of tools and practical, hands-on materials. The concrete-pictorial-abstract approach, based on research by psychologist Jerome Bruner, suggests that there are three steps (or representations) necessary for pupils to develop understanding of a concept. Reinforcement is achieved by going back and forth between these representations, which helps pupils to internalise the abstract. The 'bar model' of learning maths is an excellent example of this: it is a drawing that looks like a segment of bar, used to illustrate number relationships, and also known as a strip diagram, fraction strip or length model. Bar modelling helps children visualise multi-step word problems.

As a teaching sequence within a lesson or unit of learning, the mastery teaching approach looks something like this:

Bloom's mastery learning process

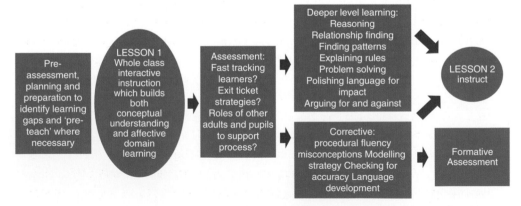

Figure 6 *Bloom's mastery learning process model works well as a pedagogical framework (adapted from Guskey, 2007)*

As a pedagogical framework, the mastery model works. In fact, it is what good teachers have always done. It does, however, highlight our need to:

- Pre-assess and pre-teach effectively so that we truly understand pupils' starting points and learning gaps before we teach.
- Recognise our need to progress learning concepts from concrete before abstract learning.
- Ensure that learning is inclusive and interactive, involving all pupils in the learning experiences.

The model also necessitates that we reconsider the ways in which we plan lessons, deploy resources and include other adults, and the pace at which we teach the curriculum content in a structured way. Factors for consideration include:

- Ensuring an expectation that every pupil reaches a minimum (but high) level of knowledge and understanding of the same content.
- A carefully sequenced, structured approach, concentrating on small steps of progression and focusing on a clear understanding of how pupils learn a subject and, in doing so, helping to avoid typical misconceptions.
- Additional support for those who need it to reach the minimum level, through corrective teaching, interventions, etc.
- A focus on learning being about pupils' ability to recall, apply and demonstrate their knowledge, understanding and skill in different contexts over a period of time.
- Regular assessment, through a variety of means (precise questioning, learning review, formative assessment and testing), which helps ensure accurate understanding of pupils' learning. (Adapted from Teaching Schools Council, 2016, p.21.)

Importantly, the successful implementation of mastery teaching means that, as schools and leaders, we need to be clear about what these practices include. Just as, for example, the London Air Ambulance team prepare for the unexpected, so too should schools be able to define core learning principles that outline the best elements of pedagogy and how we teach. Without that, we are rudderless and bound by the interpretation of mastery or any form of learning by others. Our approach to tackling this, at both Woodhill and Foxfield primary schools, was to find ways to make mastery learning visible. We created exemplification materials for expected and greater-depth standards. We captured the journeys to mastery over longer periods of time from pupils' books. We visited other schools where mastery teaching was embedded. But critically, we decided ourselves what we believed mastery of learning to be. Through meetings, discussions and debates across our schools, we took ownership of the debate and made it our own.

The importance of planning

With the revised national curriculum and subsequent assessment framework upon us, the accepted position within our education system is that to raise standards in schools we expand the concept of mastery teaching as a lever for greater equity within classrooms and to make us more competitive with international counterparts. The current Ofsted inspection handbook (2018) includes the following references:

- Introduce subject content progressively and constantly demand more of pupils.
- Teachers check pupils' understanding systematically and effectively in lessons, offering clearly directed and timely support.
- Pupils develop the capacity to learn from mistakes and they become keen learners who want to find out more. Most are willing to find out new information to develop, consolidate and deepen their knowledge, understanding and skills, both in lessons and in extra-curricular activities.
- Most pupils commit to improving their work. They are given time to apply their knowledge and understanding in new ways that stretch their thinking in a wide range of subjects, and to practise key skills.

It seems unlikely that the handbook will change until 2019, which makes it increasingly important for schools to come to terms with concepts like corrective or gap teaching.

In 2016, the Teaching Schools Council published a report on the quality of teaching in primary schools. One of the key recommendations was for schools to prioritise the ongoing development of teachers and teaching. Their recommendations included:

1 Planning is purposeful, focused on learning and has a clear objective:
   - teaching approaches that are backed by evidence and show promising signs of boosting attainment are used and their impact is monitored to ensure positive outcomes for all pupils;
   - mastery teaching approaches are properly understood and used across the curriculum for all pupils, with greater depth being used to challenge the higher attaining pupils;
   - teachers and leaders pay attention to the detail of the approaches they use, avoiding only superficial engagement.
2 Subject leaders who oversee planning and teaching across all year groups are an effective resource to improve teaching. A teacher's understanding of a subject, and how children learn that subject, is very important.
   - Many schools are using specialist staff in some subjects but at present there is no evidence that subject specialists are more effective at teaching core subjects than generalists.
   - Effective schools provide a broad and balanced curriculum, with high expectations for attainment across all subjects.

A key discussion point from the team of teachers and education experts who wrote the report was about being able to define and articulate what mastery teaching means. In the schools visited as part of the review, it was clear that whatever interpretation individual schools made, everyone within the school communities had a shared view. The report commented:

> 'Successful schools give thought to what pupils need to have achieved by the end of the school year and then plan backwards to teach the relevant skills and knowledge. This can be done without using a mastery curriculum, but taking a mastery approach leads to a more deliberately crafted "learning journey" across the academic year.' (Teaching Schools Council, 2016)

How this translates to practice necessitates a blended approach where both the teaching sequence for lessons and the longer-term skills for learning units are mapped out in advance – this is what Mark Burns and Andy Griffith articulate brilliantly in their book *Teaching Backwards* (2014). Mapping the mastery learning sequence over time begins with a secure understanding of pupils' starting points and knowledge of the learning objectives to teach and then recalibrating these into a learning sequence where the aims and ambitions for the learning culminate in a planned outcome. It is teaching that enables learners to move from novice to expert, or apprentice to master.

Because the mastery model specifically requires teachers to teach concepts and skills in a structured, progressive order, it makes us more aware of the need to 'pre-teach' pupils the knowledge required to make progress and the need to know every learner's starting point before embarking on a learning sequence. For example, you cannot teach conversions of 24-hour time to 12-hour time unless all pupils have a grasp of what time is or how the hours on a clock are constructed. This places assessment *for* learning at the heart of mastery, rather than assessment *of* learning. It also raises the status of corrective teaching

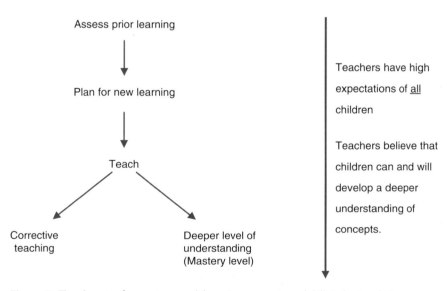

Figure 7 *The planning for mastery model requires concepts and skills to be taught in a progressive order*

for pupils struggling with a concept, giving them more time to consolidate learning. For this to happen, we need to see the struggles of learning alongside success and make more time to unpick the learning failures.

Instead of giving children separate, disconnected learning tasks that we perceive they can do, we need to provide more opportunities for pupils to make mistakes and support each other to understand the value of failure. In the Polish education system, young people are expected to fail (Ripley, 2014). Learning is deliberately challenging and hard. The logic makes sense. If the learning is hard, routine failure is the only way to learn. Just as Daniel Coyle (2010) describes climbing the ice mountain, so too does John Hattie make a similar point about the benefits of outdoor learning centres: success is going from failure to failure without losing your enthusiasm.

Some key considerations

Here are some key considerations when planning for mastery and deepening learning.

1   What are the incremental steps to the final learning outcome or learning goal that we aspire to?

2   What are the starting points for different groups?

3   What feedback might we give the learner to enable quality next steps?

4   How do we design learning experiences that will enable learners to:
   • see what the final expectations for learning look like?
   • safely explore and practise the learning in multiple ways?
   • gain mastery over the learning through application to another context?
   • evaluate their learning and sense achievement?

The talent myth

For our current generation of learners, there is a paradox: accomplishment is defined more by pace and ease of journey than by a sense of satisfaction in completing a job well done – however difficult the journey. Just 30 years ago, it was not uncommon for children to have a paper round, work part-time on a Saturday or offer to help within the family to earn money. There was an understanding that patience, hard work and effort were valuable character traits in any person and that these principles would guide us in making better decisions about our futures.

Take *The X Factor* as an example of modern-day thinking. We view the rise to stardom of individuals over eight weeks – watch them blossom from our living rooms, gliding through each episode, riding on their innate ability and genius. We pay thanks to those individuals who gave such prodigies a chance to prove themselves – for unearthing raw talent. The story is always one of discovery rather than practice. We view the performance but not the rehearsal. These are what Matthew Syed (2015) describes as 'talent myths'.

David Hockney's exhibition at Bradford's Cartwright Hall provides a profoundly visual exploration of this learning journey – exposing the talent myth as false. Representing a mixed collection of his work, spanning his entire career, Hockney exposes himself as a painter, draughtsman, printmaker, stage designer and photographer. Critically, we see Hockney the novice and not Hockney the expert. His work inspires, not just because of his bold use of colour and playful style, but also because of his commitment to mastery as a journey instead of a finished piece. This commitment presents itself through his experimentation with different media and adventure within different artistic mediums. The journey of his craft displaces the final finished piece in significance. Viewed through this lens, the practice becomes as or more important than the performance.

The Cartwright Hall exhibition demonstrates Hockney's commitment to every single art form. His early work is reminiscent of other great artists, from whom he was not afraid to borrow inspiration. He describes his immersion in artistic processes as his most powerful tool, alluding to his love and passion for learning. Reflecting on his experiences at Bradford Grammar School, Hockney reminds us of the need to connect learning experiences with meaning and the joy of feeling like a learner: 'I was interested in everything at first. I loved it all, it was thrilling to be at grammar school where I knew I would enjoy everything they asked me to do.'

The paradox of mastery learning, then, is that one can be both expert and novice at the same time. Hockney has never been afraid of embracing new technologies or reinventing himself, allowing his art to remain in a state of flux. The possibilities for learning are as much about mindset as they are about expertise, which is maybe why, at 80 years old, Hockney is still as prolific as he has always been. For our current generation of learners, accomplishment is defined more by the pace and ease of success than by a sense of satisfaction in completing a job well done. Instant gratification has replaced the concept of work ethic, where success is hard-fought and gained over time. Once a virtue, patience in attaining a desired goal has become as rare as handwritten letters. This paradox compels us to compete to perform, rather than collaborate to learn – to frame success within the race to complete a task, as opposed to valuing the quality of a genuine learning outcome. It has impacted on our relationships, how we view the process of learning, our ability to accept failure and our own mental health.

Mastering something

Photo 14 shows a wonderful example all of the elements of mastery, where learning improvements have evolved over time through the process of deliberate practice of skills, learning through multiple mistakes and refining actions, modifying behaviours and beliefs along the way. Mastery has provided our most successful model for learning for millennia across the world. It gave us the wonderful composers of nineteenth-century Vienna and the artists of the Italian Renaissance. But these examples are not restricted to cognitive domain learning alone. In all of the examples, the relationship with the learning tasks and the attitudes developed towards the need for practice and resilience, as well as self-efficacy, have an important role to play. In his book, *The Concise Mastery*, Robert Greene (2012, p. 7) notes:

> *'What we find in the stories of great masters is essentially the following pattern: a youthful passion or predilection, a chance encounter that allows them to discover how to apply it, an apprenticeship in which they come alive with energy and focus.'*

Greene argues that mastery, in this context, is about opportunity and effort. The talent myth of ability, coupled with our twenty-first-century impatience for instant success, is a toxic combination for deep learning. So, what can we do about it?

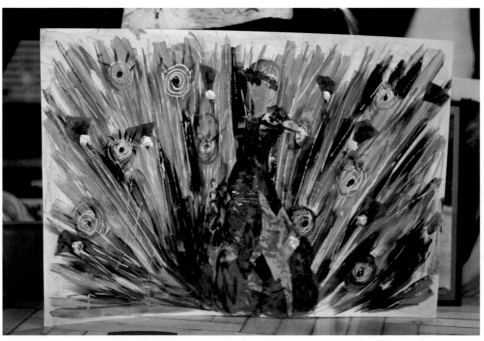

Photo 14 *Learning evolves over time through the deliberate practice of skills and the inevitable, important mistakes*

Mastery learning and the social learner

As we distil the concept of mastery into a school context, the challenge we face is balancing mastery *learning* with mastery *teaching*. While they are both equally important and interdependent, it is the theory of mastery teaching based on a theory of learning that overinflates the cognitive domain and that has come to infiltrate the language of government and Ofsted accountability, placing pressure on schools to adapt their frameworks for teaching in order to demonstrate progression. It is this misunderstanding that has blinded politicians, creating a cognitive bias and leading to our education system focusing on the wrong areas for our most persistently disadvantaged pupils.

In 2013, Michael Gove announced plans to reform the English curriculum. What he essentially wanted to introduce was a mastery model for learning. 'My new curriculum will allow my children to compete with the very best', was the headline captured by *The Daily Telegraph* (Dominiczak, 2013). Speaking to ITV's *Daybreak* programme, he said:

> *'I want my children, who are in primary school at the moment, to have the sort of curriculum that children in other countries have, which are doing better than our own. Because, when my son and daughter graduate from school and then either go on to university or into the workplace, they're competing for college places and jobs with folk from across the globe, and I want my children to receive an education as rigorous as any country's.' (As reported in the Guardian, Adams, 2013)*

The 'any other countries' included Hong Kong, Singapore and South Korea, all places with a strong instructional approach to learning, where knowledge and skills are highly prized.

While not disputing the principles of a mastery model for learning, Mr Gove's eulogy to South East Asia simplified the argument about how pupils learn in contexts where there are, historically, lower levels of social capital and less emphasis on affective domain learning.

An oversimplification of the argument

Let's take Japan as an example. According to the Organization for Economic Co-operation and Development (OECD), Japan ranks highly amongst its peers in providing its rich and poor pupils with equal educational opportunities. The OECD estimates that in Japan only about nine per cent of the variation in pupil performance is explained by pupils' socio-economic backgrounds. The graduation rate from school is over 96 per cent (a full 13 per cent more than in the US), and the attendance rates of pupils who choose to remain in lessons in the two weeks prior to the PISA testing, compared to pupils who skip lessons, are much higher in Japan than other developed countries. Only two per cent of Japanese pupils elect not to attend classes before the tests are sat. This is significant. According to the OECD:

> *'In PISA participating countries and economies, skipping a whole day of school is more common in disadvantaged schools than in advantaged schools. (Disadvantaged schools are defined as schools in the bottom quarter on the PISA index of economic, social and cultural status of schools within each country/economy.) This is observed in 44 countries and economies, including Japan, compared with only four education systems where students in advantaged schools are more likely to have skipped a day of school.' (OECD, 2015)*

Japan's low levels of pupil truancy highlight the importance that the country places on education and the value placed on learning. Japan has undertaken many of the learning reforms that we have in the UK in order to streamline curriculum, and it places high emphasis on a mastery model for learning, but they also have a cultural expectation where affective domain matters too. For example, Japanese pupils will often work collaboratively on problem-solving tasks, and more-able pupils will take responsibility for supporting pupils who are struggling. We saw a similar response from pupils at both Woodhill and Foxfield as soon as we began to alter the curriculum model, ensuring that more trips, visits and coherent learning sequences were planned that connected classroom learning to broader experiences. Attendance rose from below national levels to almost 97 per cent. The message? Lessons have to be worthy of attending.

During the 2015 PISA tests, when questioned about attitudes to learning in science, Japanese pupils were found to have average intrinsic motivation (pupils learn science because they love the subject) but, critically, significantly higher levels of instrumental motivation (an understanding that science can be useful in the future). The report also concluded that Japanese pupils had higher levels of self-efficacy (belief in one's ability to succeed in specific situations or accomplish a task), which they put down to positive feedback received from teachers, peers and parents, and the positive emotions associated with that feedback.

In other words, the focus on a mastery approach to teaching alone has not been the defining success of Japan's reduction in gaps between more and less able pupils. Instead, Japan has created a learning-centred culture where pupils:

- understand the value of learning
- view learning as a collaborative process
- connect learning in school with future employment opportunities.

These are all learning traits that shift beyond the cognitive domain. The relationship with the learning journey matters as much as the stuff-of-learning content and approaches to teaching.

What are Japan doing so right?

But there is something else going on in Japan that is having a huge impact on reducing the gaps between most and least advantaged pupils. Writing in August 2017, Alana Semuels took a closer look at the OECD report about Japan's success. In an article titled 'Japan might be what equity in education might look like', she describes the devastation of the Fukushima nuclear power plant disaster of 2011 and its impact on the relocation of families and their education system:

'Piles of contaminated soil, covered up, still dot the landscape, and many homes are shuttered. The local primary school has just 51 students, compared to more than 200 before the accident. Yet the quality of education given to returnees is top-notch. The government built a new school

for students outside the radiation zone, in a town called Kawamata, and though the classes are still very small – first grade has only two students – the school is well staffed. In a classroom I visited, all five second-graders in the school watched a teacher demonstrate flower-arranging as three other teachers surrounded them, helping them with each step. In another, a math teacher quizzed students on odd and even numbers, and as the students split into groups to discuss a problem on the board, another teacher leaned in to help.'

Many of the students returning to areas hit hardest by the disaster of 2011 are from single-parent families and have suffered significant financial hardship. However, the federal government has gone to great lengths to ensure that equality within education is valued as much as education standards. Pupils were given grants to ensure that they had fresh food and learning resources, but perhaps most significantly, in Japan teachers are appointed not to specific schools by schools, but to regional prefectures. This means that the strongest teachers are deployed to regions where they are needed most. This has the benefit of ensuring that teacher learning is maximised because teachers are exposed to working in different environments and have different experiences. Andreas Schleicher, from the OECD education and skills development team, said that: 'Disadvantage is really seen as a collective responsibility. There's a lot going on to redirect the better teachers, and more precious resources, towards the more disadvantaged students.' (Semuels, 2017)

Another contributing factor to Japan's ability to reduce achievement gaps is the level of autonomy that teachers are given. Japanese teachers are rewarded with a great deal of freedom in how to improve pupil outcomes. Using Lesson Study approaches, teachers research and design lessons over a set time period and then present new thinking to other teachers, who give feedback. In her article, Alana Semuels (2017) highlights how:

'Teachers join together to identify school-wide problems, and organise themselves into teams to address those problems, sometimes writing a report or publishing a book on how to solve them. It's not about an individual star teacher, but about teamwork.'

The challenges in the UK

By contrast, when the UK announced new education reforms in 2014, Mr Gove, then Secretary for the Department for Education, failed to comment on the importance of the learning dispositions and attitudes that connect learning skills to learning behaviours. It is this connection that makes it impossible to separate a mastery teaching model from a mastery learning approach. By contrast, Mr Gove was seduced by the concept of whole-class instructional teaching, which includes:

- No differentiation in content taught (differentiation occurs in the support and intervention provided to different pupils).
- The questioning and scaffolding that individual pupils receive in class as they work through problems will differ, with higher attainers challenged through more demanding problems, which deepens their knowledge of the same content.

- Rapid intervention, commonly through individual or small-group support later the same day – there are very few 'closing the gap' strategies, because there are very few gaps to close.

- Deep understanding achieved through covering fewer topics in greater depth.

Our challenge, as professionals, is to unpick what each means and then reframe both models through cognitive *and* affective domain lenses. Instead of viewing mastery learning as a teaching model alone, we should see it as a learning journey – there are greater possibilities within this subtle reframing that can help us serve all our pupils, including our most disadvantaged, in a better way?

If we defined mastery as a journey to excellence in any given domain or concept, rather than a teaching strategy for school improvement, it would be fair to argue that learning would be valued more as a collective and social experience, which has the biggest impact when connected to meaning and purpose. The work of the Behavioural Insights Team, established in 2010 by the coalition government, highlights how when learning is social, attractive and timely, it has greater traction and capacity to connect with something wider and bigger than skills and knowledge alone (Halpern, 2015). Viewed this way, mastery of learning is less a checklist of skills and more a whole-school approach to the organisation of great learning.

Tommy's story

I want to take a moment here to introduce Tommy.

Case study: Tommy

'Tommy is a climber' was one of the first exchanges I had with a member of staff, days before Foxfield Primary School was placed into special measures. It was an understatement. The oldest of two siblings, Tommy lived with his mum and step-dad in a council flat on the infamous Glyndon estate.

The Glyndon Estate is not a comfortable place to grow up. The estate featured in a documentary, *Gangland*, shown in 2016. Just making the programme proved to be so dangerous that the film producer, Paul Blake, had to revise the format, as someone was seriously hurt mid-filming. In the end, it was decided that getting the gangs to record footage of themselves was the best way forward, rather than exposing cameramen to the dangers of filming some of London's most notorious criminals. The documentary featured gang members talking openly about their lives, including seeing people stabbed, shot and fighting with police. Since the documentary was first shown, two of the members have died. There is a dark side in some communities, to which our schools offer a very contrasting environment.

In 2017, the *Evening Standard* published an article: 'Former gang member reveals hidden peril of knives on a walk through the streets of Woolwich.' It featured Sam, a former Woolwich gang member, describing life on the streets of South East London and a culture of drug dealing, gang life and knife crime, impacting so severely within a community. In the interview, Sam reveals that he has carried a knife since the age of ten and has spent more than a fifth of his life in prison. In one of his more chilling quotes, he says:

'I know this gonna sound bad but when Lee Rigby had his head chopped off outside the army barracks not far from here, us lot thought it was pretty normal. We'd seen people hacked with a machete. Set on fire. It's the norm that people you know get killed. After a while you become immune.' (Cited in Cohen, 2017)

This is the environment in which Tommy was growing up. Sometimes, after school, the boys on the estate – as young as eight and nine – play 'gangs', using pretend knives and role-playing anti-social behaviour. Staff at Foxfield Primary School had been asked by community police officers to identify these young boys from CCTV footage. There were genuine concerns that exposure to such dysfunctional, anti-social behaviour may lead to an increase in violence for the next generation.

Like many of the 'Woolwich Boys' profiled through the documentary or media, Tommy didn't see his dad too much. When he did spend an occasional weekend with him, the school knew that Mondays were going to be tough. Not that Tommy cared too much about school in 2014. The curriculum offered was dull and uninspiring, the teaching did not take into account Tommy's learning challenges or interests, and too few staff saw beyond Tommy's home situation to understand Tommy the child. So Tommy did what Tommy liked to do, and that was climb.

When Foxfield was rebuilt in 2014, they designed a large, open concrete play space, which was surrounded on two sides by residual earth banked up against the wall. This created a five-metre drop from the top of the bank, overlooking the playground. The building contractors installed a six-foot high wooden fence around the bank, with a gate at the bottom to deter pupils from climbing over and potentially falling off the five-metre wall that surrounded the play space. They failed to consider that, for pupils like Tommy, jumping over the fence and dangling off the wall offered a better alternative to staying in lessons – especially those he hated. Tommy was also inclined to scale the fence and walk along the top of the drop when he was upset or angry. It gave him control in a world where Tommy had little – especially when he found out that mum was pregnant again.

The first few weeks after new leadership arrived at Foxfield were occupied with dealing with situations involving Tommy or other pupils behaving in similar ways. Risk assessments were put in place, health and safety checks undertaken and a new, higher fence erected to deter Tommy from climbing. These are the kinds of behaviours that schools in crisis exhibit; they are reactive and strategic, what some would describe as putting one's house in order. It didn't stop Tommy from being angry, though. Like all the pupils I have ever known in Tommy's situation, he was a smart kid. He knew which teachers liked him and which staff were fair or not. What made him mad was the sense of injustice if he was treated differently, whether this meant being patronised, told off unfairly or given different work to complete – Tommy was highly tuned in to the hierarchy and status of academic achievement in the classroom. He noticed how teachers' body language shifted towards certain pupils – how some pupils' actions elicited effusive nods in agreement, while others received tacit acknowledgement of learning tasks. He was even disposed to notice the type of feedback he received in his learning books compared to other pupils – it was as if the school didn't care enough about him so he would care even less about the school, and then some!

The strategy for turning around Tommy's attitude towards school was not a conscious one but, over the next two terms, Tommy noticed subtle behaviour changes that helped him. Firstly, the school stopped arguing with mum or, even worse, avoiding her altogether, and began to engage on her level. They met regularly and listened to her. This revealed health worries she had about her expected baby and the extent to which Tommy was anxious about this. Staff learnt that Tommy wanted to speak more about the positive relationship he had with his dad and granddad, even though he didn't see them too often. This led to the school setting up structured times when Tommy could come and talk about family life. Listening to Tommy's concerns also revealed some health issues that he had. Home life wasn't always easy. His bedroom was damp and he had asthma, which flared up during specific weather conditions. This allowed the school to offer some health interventions and work more closely to help Tommy just feel a bit better about coming to school. Tommy's attendance improved and, as his behaviour got better, teachers stopped rejoicing inside when Tommy was off sick. Instead, they followed up to find out where he was.

Undoubtedly, though, what made the biggest difference for Tommy during this period was the relationship he began to form with staff. Shortly after the school was placed in special measures, the leadership team took the decision to move the leadership office away from the coded, tucked-away corridor at the front of the building, down into the bowels of the school on the ground floor. This was nearer to Tommy's classroom but also located more centrally to the dining hall, playground and other social spaces. The leadership office became an open-plan space where teachers would meet to plan or meet informally. This modelled 'open to learning' leadership but also leadership through relationships. Whether Tommy wanted to test staff or whether he was curious about the changes taking place at the school, he started to pop in quietly, always unannounced, just to say 'hello', and then he would leave. Recognising the social benefits to Tommy in these brief exchanges, staff began to engage him in conversation, firstly inquiring about family and home, then about his learning: challenges, likes, successes and those 'useful learning mistakes'. Gradually, slowly, Tommy built trust and learned to trust.

The school then put in place some structure around when Tommy could come into the leadership space. He was allowed to come in during break times, to share good learning, and when he was in crisis, Tommy was allowed to sit quietly and reflect. Just knowing that Tommy had a space that he was allowed to use to calm down made a difference. Instead of climbing the fence to walk along the wall, Tommy would come inside the leadership office and sit.

Between 2014 and 2017, these episodes of crisis became fewer and fewer. Tommy learnt to regulate his behaviour and also learnt to be a learner.

This chapter has focused on the concept of mastery of both the learning journey, including our relationship with learning, and motives to learn, being as important as mastery of subject knowledge and content. For Tommy, understanding the importance and value of learning beliefs and developing a relationship with learning was crucial to his cognitive domain learning, as we shall see.

Learning to love what you do

One of the strategies that helped Tommy turn things around in the classroom was the introduction of mixed-ability table groupings of four, where he was able to learn with other pupils and engage on equal terms in problem-solving and reasoning challenges. It was the social nature of the learning that gave Tommy confidence. He was able to participate and feel valued as a learner. Just as the Japanese place high value on more-able pupils supporting less-able ones, so too does the mixed ability KAGAN collaborative learning structure. Pupils sit in mixed ability groups of four and have face partners and shoulder partners to maximise dialogue and discussion linked to taught key teaching points. This helps pupils take joint responsibility for each other's learning, as well as their own.

Nothing helps you learn better than having opportunities to explain your thinking to others. The school also introduced a range of social learning strategies in the shape of sentence stems so that Tommy and other children could develop an extensive vocabulary for social learning (see Photo 15).

It is the social nature of communication, coupled with the drive to make sense of the world, that leads to understanding and, eventually, meaning. Learning in itself is worthless without the social dimension in which we develop a common framework for understanding. This includes a clear reason to learn and a strong purpose for learning, which connects skills with 'why'. In order to reason, persuade and debate, pupils need a considerable amount of practice and experience in learning conversations. The social dimension of learning has value and currency because of the interaction and meaning co-constructed between teachers, groups of learners and individual learners. This is not to say that thinking time or processing does not have an important role within learning, nor am I suggesting that muscle memory does not play a critical role within the learning process. Our working memories are notoriously fickle, which is why we are reliant on the social nature of learning and non-cognitive traits to transfer learning to the permanence of long-term memory. Our working memory only retains a small number of slots (seven being the magic number) to hold different sets of information and knowledge. International studies focusing on our capacity to remember information without practising highlight that up to 45% of new learning can be lost if we fail to repeat learning tasks through deliberate practice. Our memory retention rates can be affected in just 20 minutes if we do not continuously return to learning concepts with opportunities to practise skills. Just as with talent myths, it isn't the case that some people are born with great memories. It is just that they practise harder to ensure

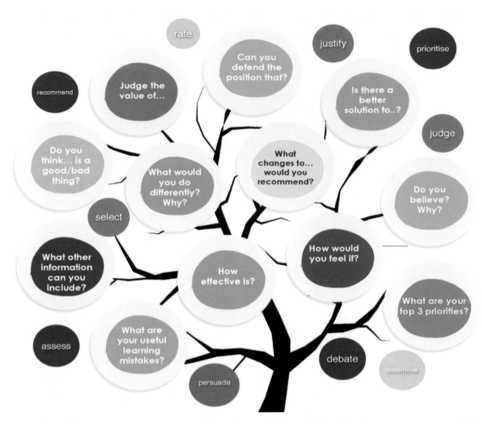

Photo 15 *Social learning strategies in the form of sentence stems help to develop an extensive vocabulary*

working memory information is committed to long-term memory through repetition and by forming strong relationships with the learning.

The neuroplasticity of our brains means that our capacity to learn and remember skills is not fixed but has a better opportunity to grow from focused practice alongside opportunities to socialise learning experiences. When we plan for deliberate practice using a consistent approach and with consistent levels of repetition, we have a much higher chance of remembering information. Until something is secured fully into long-term memory, we need to practise multiple times within a short time span. The best way to do this is to ensure that the practice is connected to a social experience that has meaning. This maximises our potential for co-constructing new learning (amending our thinking along the way) and connecting old learning with new learning.

Every one of us is the product of learning that is co-constructed over time as a social experience, honed and crafted through deliberate or accidental practice, fuelled by multiple opportunities to make errors, slipping and sliding along the way. Think about your best and most powerful learning experience as a teacher and track its journey from concept to reality. Most of us will share experiences of learning that are inherently social exchanges. Quite often, too, these experiences are opportunistic. Despite what we may think about how we learn, our best learning is least likely to take place in formal settings and most likely to become memorable through the social encounter as a process of constructing meaning. All of this strengthens the case to ensure that the balance of the learning hierarchy moves closer towards non-cognitive domain learning traits.

Measuring and capturing mastery

The challenge, therefore, if mastery is based on both experience and opportunity, is how we measure or capture this. Let's take a leadership example. Leadership successes are less defined by singular moments or an epiphany but, more likely, by a multitude of small marginal gains, hard-won over time by an awareness of our need to learn from error-analysis. It is the near-miss landing conversations that lead to incremental improvement over time rather than a proclamation of action. Interrogation of failure makes failure data-rich.

But this doesn't square with the narrative of improvement that we like to tell ourselves. We are afflicted by a multitude of biased behaviours (cultural and social) that reframe our belief system about our own self-importance and impact. This includes:

- Hindsight bias – once we have all the facts, it is easy to see what the correct course of action should have been.

- Hierarchy bias – we are inclined to defer to the views of those more senior within our working environment, believing that rank and status bring accuracy of thinking.

- Group think – we are more likely to assume that those within our own group are correct and have ability rather than those outside of our group.

- Cognitive dissonance – the belief that we are right and refusal to acknowledge contrary evidence.

We tell the narrative of leadership successes pretty much as a football commentator recalls a great football match. We inflate the importance of moments that fit our schema and we exaggerate our own infallible wisdom so that it tells the story of improvement we want people to hear. The outcome of this becomes a tale where mastery or excellence becomes less about the marginal gains won and more about the individual talent or aptitude: the surgeon who performs the lifesaving operation or the soldier who mows down the opposition before planting the flag in triumph.

By contrast, mastery learning is complex, bound by social encounters – opportunities to fail and learn from multiple mistakes. True mastery is not something easy to quantify because it is bound by the networks we form and relationships with people. No wonder, then, that the misunderstanding of a mastery approach to learning has slipped towards knowledge and skills instead of a blended approach where affective domain traits are also valued. Imagine a world where social learning, struggle and practice are valued as the prized assets of deep learning. It would certainly provide us with a more creative, resilient and collaborative framework for learning.

Case study: Tommy

Tommy was not a whole-brain thinker. He was impulsive, reactive, emotional and, sometimes, explosive. He was using a part of his brain that Ned Herrmann describes as 'relational'. Tommy was overdependent on his instinctive and intuitive skill-set when dealing with challenges. His instinctive way of thinking led him to overreact or misinterpret social cues when processing information around him. In many ways, the type of education that Tommy received before 2014 also reinforced the message about his learning potential. He found school uninteresting, felt judged and labelled. Learning tasks were often low-skill-level, repetitive worksheets, he was placed in the lowest ability group for most of the day and he found the overemphasis on the core business of reading, writing and maths unappealing to his interests outside of school. Neither he nor the school had managed to see a more expansive way of organising learning that simultaneously complemented his skills and developed his weaknesses.

By contrast, whole-brain learners can see the bigger picture. Learning has currency because it can be applied beyond school. They see patterns and make connections between learning domains. They also recognise that while different tasks require different mental processes, and different people prefer different kinds of thinking, learning is more fun and meaningful when teams of learners strategically leverage the full spectrum of thinking available.

In 2014, Tommy was given a chance to celebrate his whole-brain learning. One of the key recommendations in the disastrous Foxfield Ofsted report concerned the lack of ambition that pupils felt about learning and work. In response to this, the school revised the way in which decision-making and leadership drove school improvement. The school established a Parent Forum, which met fortnightly to review key elements of school improvement. They made public the extent to which the school was failing its community and gave responsibility to families for solving the challenges. The forum initiated change to how they communicated, supported changes to the way in which phonics and Early Years teaching were organised and promoted the development of pupil voice and pupil leadership.

A Junior Leadership Team (JLT) was created and children given responsibility to lead change across the school. They wrote an action plan that included taking responsibility for supporting school self-evaluation. They received training in looking for good learning in school and worked with school leaders to support book looks, lesson observations and other leadership tasks. At the same time, the school appointed its own pupil workforce. Positions were advertised and the JLT coordinated the application process. Jobs were established with responsibility for the environment, pupil behaviour, gardening, friendship, coordinating social games and school improvement. The JLT also worked with school leadership to develop a programme of work experience for older pupils. They organised a careers fair where professionals spoke about the importance of school-based learning skills and their use in the wider workplace. Pupils went on visits to the local university, worked with the Woolwich Barracks Armed Forces team and developed a programme of non-cognitive domain skills training. This included mindfulness and wellbeing training, sailing skills and even sword fencing.

Simultaneously, the arts and physical development were prioritised across the school so that pupils' broader learning experiences were developed. Specialist teachers were appointed and the provision for teaching across the curriculum ensured that children like Tommy were given an opportunity to broaden their interests in a range of learning areas. Pupils learnt to value themselves as learners with a vision. They began to articulate how school-based learning could be used in other aspects of life. They were taking responsibility for their own learning but that of each other as well. When Ofsted returned to the school in September 2015, they highlighted:

- Pupils told inspectors that they take 'a piece of the school home' with them 'which helps them to reflect on their learning'. This comment typically illustrates daily teaching which pupils also said includes, 'coaching each other', 'generating questions for hot-seating', and being 'involved in lessons because they are not simply sitting down plonked on a chair'. Teachers provide pupils with the opportunity to tell them what they like and dislike about their teaching. These features are prevalent and contribute to pupils learning extremely well.

- The strong emphasis on raising aspirations means that Year 5 and 6 pupils are given an early start to thinking about their future. Pupils are highly ambitious and the school encourages them, as the first generation in their families, to think about higher education. Established links with the University of Greenwich, careers fayre and work-shadowing are used effectively to give pupils a sound start to thinking about their lives in the future.

- Pupils have a mature understanding of taking on responsibilities as mentors, monitors and as elected ambassadors on the school council and the primary leadership programme. They acquit themselves very well in these roles and use the process to learn about principles of representation and speaking out in a democracy. (Ofsted, 2015)

Tommy left primary school in 2017, having achieved the expected standard in reading, writing and maths. More importantly, he left primary school as a learner, with a toolkit of experience and a newfound love of learning, which will serve him well.

Key messages

1 The concept of mastery learning, where pupils 'master' core learning components sequentially and progressively, must be balanced with the need to value broader learning traits that are reflective of non-cognitive domain.

2 Disadvantaged pupils are more likely to suffer if we persist with a narrow curriculum that places higher emphasis on mastery of knowledge and skills. This will not close gaps between the most and least advantaged pupils, because attitudes to learning affect heavily our willingness and capacity to learn.

3 International achievement comparisons have created a false narrative about how pupils in the highest-performing PISA charts make better progress. Incorrectly, we have taken elements of the mastery teaching sequence used in Singapore, China and Japan, without fully recognising the importance of other factors that close gaps and increase social equity.

4 Examples from both business and education support the view that, internationally, we need to provide a more expansive framework for learning, which values mastery of learning dispositions alongside mastery of learning skills, increases motivation to learn and connects learning with a deeper sense of purpose.

Key questions to consider:

1 Does your school have the double understanding of a mastery teaching sequence and the mastery journey of learning over time?

2 How does your school promote reasoning and language development alongside mastery so that pupils can articulate their thinking more deeply?

3 How does your curriculum make time for pupils to practise and embed skills over time?

4 To what extent do pupils support each other to master key skills?

5 How do you make visible core expectations for both staff and pupils in relation to mastering curriculum content?

If mastery learning is defined by the need for deliberate practice, deep learning, reflection and the application of taught skills, then feedback has to focus more on provocative prompts than procedural fluency. This necessitates that we look again at the purpose of assessment in order for pupils to be better able to evaluate, challenge and respond to those 'useful learning mistakes'. The language of evaluation needs to be taught explicitly and modelled before children are able to use it fluently to evaluate their own learning. This is expansive assessment, which we will examine further in the next chapter.

8 Expansive assessment

Expansive assessment ensures that accurate information about pupils' learning is used wisely at classroom level to help teachers and learners precision-plan incremental gains that match learning needs. Key strategies for developing formative assessment include:

1   Clarifying, understanding and sharing learning objectives.

2   Developing a clear curriculum philosophy.

3   Engineering effective classroom discussions, tasks and activities that elicit evidence of learning. This includes promoting classroom discourse and interactive whole-class teaching.

4   Providing feedback that moves learners forward.

5   Activating pupils as a *learning resource* for one another, including collaborative learning, reciprocal teaching and peer-assessment.

6   Activating pupils as *owners* of their own learning in terms of metacognition, motivation, interest, attribution and self-assessment.

Expansive assessment maximises learning relationships so that learning for both children and teacher enables a better understanding of how taught skills, feedback and specific misconceptions lead to deliberate practice, precision-planned next steps and greater challenge. It creates agency amongst pupils to own a 'useful learning mistake' as a new opportunity to reflect and engage more deeply with new learning, which builds on error-analysis. It creates a language for learning that pupils can use to justify, explain and make sense of choices made in learning tasks. In other words, it is assessment that is used formatively, and it actively informs pedagogy and meta-cognition.

Education research from John Hattie (2008) provides conclusive evidence that the quality of feedback in learning plays a pivotal role in ensuring that pupils make good progress and learn well. However, feedback in itself is not enough to trigger modifications in learning unless it is actionable, specific and given in a helpful way. The work of Ron Berger (2003) and Carol Dweck (2017) identifies that creating a school-wide culture of giving, receiving and acting upon feedback promotes resilience, builds confidence and enables pupils to develop a 'growth mindset'.

The key to a successful formative assessment strategy is the involvement of pupils in owning their learning and each other's learning. The role of teacher becomes facilitator of learning, using all available information about pupils to guide the learning so that objectives are achieved. They do this by clarifying objectives and success criteria and by making high expectations visible. Critically, expert teachers also engineer highly effective discussions, tasks and activities, which help pupils to support each other to maximise collective support. Given that our pupils are our biggest learning resource, when taught how to give and receive feedback they are much better able to engage in a constructive dialogue, which ensures learning successes.

At Foxfield, our maths leader coordinated a project to teach pupils to develop greater reasoning skills in order to support independent and group learning in maths. Working with a team of teachers, they developed maths reasoning prompts (see Photos 16 and 17 and then taught pupils how to use them when reflecting on learning mistakes and next steps. This not only provided opportunities for reasoning, noticing patterns and making connections, but also allowed them to make choices about where to take their learning. Because the prompts demanded high levels of engagement, what could be seen as a restrictive task became a high-ceiling activity.

Problems with top-down accountability

In stark contrast, one of the most destructive consequences of an education system driven by a 'proving' agenda instead of an 'improvement' agenda is the way in which assessment is used selectively to justify cavalier and reckless education reform. For too long, assessment has been designed to work for external accountability rather than for teachers and pupils. It has created a reactive approach to school improvement and perpetuated a false narrative about what constitutes excellence in our schools. This has encouraged schools to game the system and increased pressure on leaders to exploit a strategic approach to improvement, instead of cultivating a deep learning philosophy based on design and architecture. Schools have been preoccupied with data-reporting for external accountability instead of focusing on how quality formative assessment can be used to maximise learning.

Setting national or local education targets based on rank position in international tests, rather than on specific standards achieved, defies everything we know about how pupils learn. Rank position and league tables are inappropriate as a goal for improvement, because they can be influenced by quite small differences in cohort scores. Such differences may not, in themselves, represent meaningful learning or skill differences, which should be the main focus. Despite these concerns, evaluating school success or national performance by headline data appeals to those who see improving educational outcomes as a competitive sport.

Dr Stuart Kime (Director of Education, Evidence Based Education) argues:

'How can anyone hope to become skilled in the craft of great assessment when its role in education is so mercurial and politicised, and deep understanding of it so thin on the ground

by virtue of such limited high-quality training and long-term support? Assessment has become synonymous with marking, and marking has become a proxy for effective teaching. The potential power of classroom assessment has been diminished the more it has shape-shifted its way between being a learning tool and an accountability instrument. Without recalibrating our expectations of what these valuable tools can – and cannot do – we stand little chance of harnessing assessment's true power to enhance learning.' (Kime, 2017)

This is what Martin Lindstrom (2016) differentiates as 'big data'. Big data is headline-grabbing, identifies patterns and trends between pupil outcomes and strives to provide answers for school leaders and policymakers in evaluating performance. The problem is that, while big data may be a good way to identify trends, it fails to provides answers to the causes – information about improving teaching and learning, pupil motivations and relationships between staff and pupils. As the likes of Dylan Wiliam have argued for a long time, investment in formative assessment strategies is more likely to improve the quality of education than standardised tests. It strengthens collective autonomy, by giving teachers more independence to interpret school-based evidence, and empowers pupils by involving them in the process of reflection and evaluating learning. Obsessively testing pupils has guided us away from our North Star.

International picture

Across the globe, education decision-makers are reforming school policy based on test outcomes and international databases, without really understanding the nuance of genuine school improvement. David Laws, the former Liberal Democrat MP and Treasury Chief Secretary, speaking to *The Guardian* in 2017, reflected that education policymaking during his time as a cabinet member was poor:

'A lot of decision making is not based on evidence but on hunch. I had little coming to me from civil servants that presented the latest academic evidence. Too often, they just serve up practical advice about how the minister can do what he or she wants. But politicians are prone to make decisions based on ideology and personal experience.' (Cited in Wilby, 2017)

In reality, education outcomes will always vary because they are cohort-dependent and continuously subject to examination changes. PISA indicators merely simplify and quantify top-line information about outcomes. Because the PISA data sets are made public and expanded to more than 60 participating countries, the data provided has placed policy-leaders under pressure to maintain and increase improvement trends. In Australia, for example, they have set themselves the target to reach the top five performing nations by 2025. This response followed their significant decline in reading performance between 2000 and 2009.

PROVE WITH A DRAWING

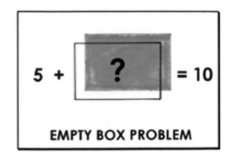

$5 + \boxed{?} = 10$

EMPTY BOX PROBLEM

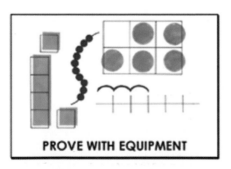

MATHS STORY

EXPLAIN IT!

STEP BY STEP

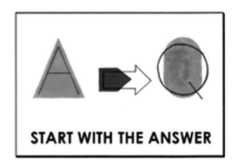

START WITH THE ANSWER

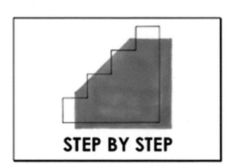

PROVE WITH EQUIPMENT

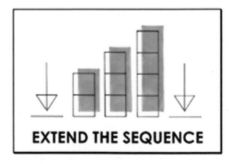

EXTEND THE SEQUENCE

Photos 16 and 17 *Feedback prompts developed by maths leaders helped pupils to develop greater reasoning skills in maths*

PATTERN SPOTTER

ERROR SPOTTER

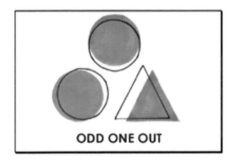

ODD ONE OUT

COACHING

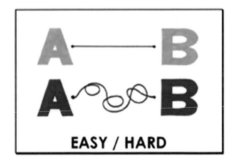

EASY / HARD

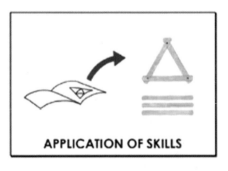

APPLICATION OF SKILLS

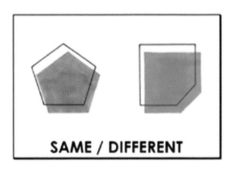

SAME / DIFFERENT

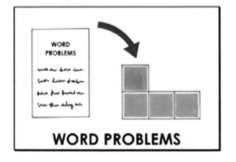

WORD PROBLEMS

We have seen the impact of this in the UK, where rank-chasing reforms have led to simplistic, headline-grabbing initiatives. Quick fixes have replaced sustainable, incremental growth, forcing schools to focus exponentially on limited indicators of success, rather than 'small data'. As we have already suggested, our addiction to policy reform has been based on whim and hunch, instead of practitioner-driven evidence. *The Economist* (2010) headlined 'An international report card: Shanghai's school students out-perform all others' but failed to report that Shanghai's education system is highly selective. It includes data from pupils who have retaken exams or are bussed in from elsewhere in the country. Simon Breakspear (2014, p. 3) argues:

'What educational outcomes we measure, and how we measure them, affects our understanding of the performance of our systems and policy action that is taken for improvement. The vast majority of analysis and debate in the field of whole system reform is centred on how to improve the means of educational change. Too often the ends of education – and their measurement – are assumed.'

What's gone wrong?

Twenty years of reducing assessment to outcomes and outputs has had a significant impact on leadership in schools. It has created an illusion that progress and achievement occur in linear fashion and can be tracked forensically. Our focus has drifted towards finding new and elaborate ways to measure targets rather than pupils' learning and the influence of teaching. Leadership energies have centred on the leadership progress review meeting instead of improving classroom practice, working collaboratively to enhance teaching quality and pupil experience. This has reinforced the mindset that leadership occurs in headteachers' offices rather than when they talk with children and teachers about improving practice.

Likewise, performance management targets have reinforced the message that pupils are products and that learning occurs simply by being more ambitious with targets and tracking progress. We see the grade but not the child and certainly not the learning journey, which is often unpredictable, beset with failure and multiple learning mistakes. As Graham Nuthall points out in *The Hidden Lives of Learners* (2007), there are significant gaps in any school self-evaluation framework that does not focus on the perspective of the learner. If we want to better understand how teachers craft and shape pupil learning, we must begin with individual pupils' starting points and explore just how they learn best.

The overemphasis on summative data has also led to reduced collaboration between schools and greater variance between regional performance. Not only have we witnessed the emergence of the education VIPs, but big data has also engineered a view that our education challenges are located in specific areas. This feeds the false belief that education policy is all fine, if only all areas could implement it properly. The problem this creates is one where:

1 We look to replicate the success of one location across a broader landscape, ignoring the unique characteristics and demography of each location.

2 We create the 'Matthew effect', which reinforces the parable of talent, leading to the richer schools getting richer while the poor schools just get poorer.

In an education context, the 'Matthew effect' was developed by Robert Merton (1968) to explain how eminent scientists will often get more credit than a comparatively unknown researcher, even if their work is similar. He gave an example of the disproportionate visibility given to articles from acknowledged authors at the expense of equally valid or superior articles written by unknown authors. He also noted the disproportionate impact that this can have on confidence and self-assurance. In other words, the exposure given to acknowledged scientists becomes a self-fulfilling prophecy.

The Matthew effect can also be applied to the school inspection process. We have our Ofsted 'rich' schools and our Ofsted 'poor' schools. These have been defined largely on the premise that the big data does not lie – that the Ofsted rich schools must have better teaching because outcomes are strong. Alex Quigley (2016) distinguishes that:

> 'Those "Ofsted rich" schools tend to have a more affluent and "word rich" student catchment, with low FSM [free school meals] numbers, above average results and relatively stable staffing. Alternatively, "Ofsted poor" schools are constrained by a more diverse catchment, results that are perilously close to the raised floor standards and annual difficulties with unstable staffing. Every school leader of "Ofsted poor" schools I have met recently details the interminably long action plans that consume the time of everybody to complete quick-fixes that distract from the deeper changes required. Teachers in Ofsted poor schools get invariably crushed under compliance measures related to planning and marking – a sure-fire recipe for teacher burnout.'

In other words, big data only tells part of a story, and can often perpetuate a problem rather than provide solutions. School context matters and we need to reposition how we use data to ensure that we capture the broadest possible picture – not least to properly acknowledge the amazing work that takes place in some of our most challenged schools. The poverty of language in poorer communities can have a crippling effect on some children's abilities to engage effectively in learning. It is too easy for inspectors to focus on the impact of this rather than what schools are doing to combat its effects.

London, for example, is heralded as a success story. The Commission on Inequality in Education report (Social Market Foundation, 2017) highlights that GCSE performance at age 16 across England reveals marked disparities between regions, with over 60 per cent of pupils in London achieving five good GCSEs (including English and maths) compared to 55 per cent in the West and East Midlands. At age 11, Yorkshire and Humberside and the West Midlands have disproportionately high numbers of low-scoring pupils. By contrast, the North West and London have disproportionately high numbers of high-scoring pupils.

The problem with reducing the argument to a regional challenge is that it again fails to tackle the need to examine more closely how teaching and learning are organised at classroom level. It shifts the lens away from teacher practice to leadership and accountability. No doubt the two are intrinsically linked, but highlighting the achievement gap in itself does nothing to find bespoke solutions.

Isolated and vulnerable, Ofsted poor schools can become trapped – more likely to become inward-looking, more susceptible to seduction of snake oil offered by unscrupulous education prospectors. These are schools where salvation comes at a price – the curriculum constricts even further, leaders take more drastic approaches to tightening accountability and data walls decorate school corridors, reducing pupils to colour-coded 'on track' or not. The education labels become self-fulfilling prophecies, and we lose sight of the child.

In such schools, survival depends on compliance, hierarchy and coercion. The overriding mentality is one where data is received as truth; where teaching is viewed as a science rather than an art; where progress occurs in straight lines. Teachers and schools are penalised for discrepancies between data and predictions, as though progress can be evaluated objectively through flightpaths and spreadsheet-tracking. The irony is that we have more opportunity and capacity than ever to capture a wider range of information about pupils' performance across the domains of learning, including attitudes to learning, learning strengths and learning needs.

The more we learn about the psychology of learning and the importance of aligning cognitive with non-cognitive traits, the greater the significance becomes of ensuring that high-quality, ethical assessment is paired with the teaching of wider life skills. We continue to ignore recommendations from global leaders and educationalists about the breadth of qualities needed to be successful in a complex world. We have created a high-stakes environment where one's identity as a learner resides within a narrow set of performance indicators.

An alternative

Imagine an alternative vision for assessment where we prize resilience, confidence, creativity, collaboration and teamwork alongside pupil attainment. It wouldn't be too difficult to develop a 'small data' mentality to assessment, where learning traits were valued at least as much as hard pupil outcomes. It would reveal so much more about our pupils, providing teachers with crucial information about learning characteristics, as well as their strengths and areas for development in learning domains. It would also encourage teachers to teach non-cognitive domain skills alongside formal knowledge. This is exactly what global leaders have been calling for. Table 12 shows an alternative framework for evaluating learning skills. How wonderful would it be if our profession was able to measure and evaluate success against these qualities instead of narrow, reductive data sets?

In the 'What makes great assessment?' forum publication, Dame Alison Peacock describes the current and future assessment challenges that we face in uncertain times, where:

'Too often in Key Stage 1 and Key Stage 2, confidence about teachers' own judgement and assessment erodes in favour of external test materials. It is as though the skills of detailed observation and planned learning that builds on the children's current knowledge are lost as the curriculum becomes more formal. Yet the skill of assessing what has been understood is fundamental to good planning. How can we know what to teach tomorrow if we do not know what has been understood today?' (Cited in Kime et al., 2017, p. 20)

She identifies the key assessment challenges as:

- Hyper-accountability induced by inspection and the fear this creates
- Potential introduction of a baseline test in Foundation
- Meeting the demands of national curriculum tests at the end of Key Stage Two where the 'expected' standard has been raised
- Confusion between tracking and assessment. Schools that require teachers to provide so-called 'data-drops' every few weeks, risk putting energy in the wrong place
- Further pressure from families if KS2 predicted results are linked to selective secondary school places
- Difficulty of 'proving' progress within and between year groups
- Assessment of children with SEND.

In August 2017, the *TES* published an article written by primary headteacher Ann Lyons, who also questions both the reliability of outcomes-focused summative data and its validity in being a measure of excellence. We are in the embarrassing position where the government set a minimum goal (floor standard) for 65 per cent of pupils to reach the benchmark of 'expected' standards, with only 61 per cent of pupils in the English education system achieving them. This, Ann Lyons argues, diverts attention away from the broader successes that schools are achieving, some against remarkable odds, creating further anxiety in schools. Depressingly, Ann Lyons reflects:

'I'm quite happy to be kept awake at night trying to think up practical solutions to real problems felt by actual pupils. That's my job. I'm less happy to be losing sleep about whether a narrow set of data measures could have dire consequences for my school, my staff and, frankly, my career.'

An unintended consequence of our overemphasis on outcomes as a measure of a school's worth is that the learning-centred leadership we need now more than ever buckles under the weight of test-based accountability, rather than trust-based accountability.

Table 12 The learning dispositions continuum provides an alternative framework for evaluating learning skills

	Definition	Emerging	Developing	Highly accomplished	Embedded excellence
Questions	*A way of finding out*	I don't ask too many questions	I can answer 'shallow' questions	I use a wider range of questions – 'shallow' and 'deep' to find information	I constantly ask questions to seek further information and deepen my understanding
Reflection	*Thinking about and looking back on the learning to decide how it went and where to next*	I am not sure what reflection is and what it means but I do want to learn more about this	I am reflecting on my learning with support or prompts – e.g. question starters or feedback marking	I know reflection is an important part of the learning process. I can talk about when, what and how I reflect	I understand reflection helps me with my learning. I use it continuously across a range of situations
Thinking	*Reasoning about, reflecting or pondering*	I don't usually think much during the learning and do not make connections between areas of learning	With support, I can use thinking organisers and strategies to further my learning	I can use various thinking tools and strategies to deepen my thinking and learning	I naturally select the most appropriate thinking tool and strategy to reach a decision, outcome, solution or situation I am faced with
Connections	*Linking knowledge together to create new understanding*	I find it hard to make connections or links but I am ready to learn about this	I can sometimes make connections, often with support or modelling. Sometimes I have an 'ah ha' moment and I see a link or connection	I make many links and connections between pieces of knowledge to create new ideas or deepen understanding	I constantly look for and use knowledge to connect with old and new learning to develop new understanding. I can talk about this and share with others

Determination	*The ability to stick at a challenge task when you feel like giving up. The desire and determination to self-improve and succeed*	If things are too tricky I often give up. Sometimes I don't and I want to have more determination	I can self-talk to show determination with tasks that are a little trickier and I can self-motivate to keep going	I have a number of strategies that help me to be determined when tasks are challenging. I can give examples of these	I am determined to self-improve to achieve my very best. I choose from a range of strategies to overcome obstacles and problem-solve. I identify and commit to achieving next learning steps
Self-awareness	*Aware of yourself as a learner – your actions, thoughts, strengths and next steps*	I am not sure of the things that might help me to become a better learner but I do want to know more about this	I am beginning to build awareness of what I need to do to become a better learner. I can identify some next steps to improve	I am self-aware in my actions and reflection to improve and develop my strengths. I independently work towards achieving my next steps	I am conscious of what makes me 'tick' (strengths, next steps, thoughts and personality traits). I am self-motivated and self-aware of actions I need to improve as a learner
Wonder	*To be amazed at something; the desire to know something*	I am not sure what it means to 'wonder' but there are some things I am really interested in	I sometimes wonder and imagine	I can wonder about ideas and imagine possibilities from one or two perspectives	I wonder to come up with ideas about what 'might be' from many different perspectives. I can elaborate these ideas and come up with ideas. I can distinguish between wonderings I can act on and wonderings that are unobtainable

Ethical leadership is never an end in itself and is always characterised by an overarching belief system connected to a broader set of goals. Ethical leaders are authentic leaders because they believe that what they do carries a noble prize where everyone succeeds. They create followers who share their values and they identify with the communities they lead because they see the whole person rather than a test score. They understand the importance of relationships. The unquestioned pressures of accountability, fuelled by filling the buckets of assessment results, have tested the resolve of our most diligent school leaders to hold firm to what they believe in. By contrast, the worship of narrow data has created the cult of celebrity headteachers. These are the education VIPs, who retell the false narrative of rapid improvement, failing to see the limitations and unsustainability of their approach. Viewed purely through the lens of high-stakes assessment, these heads became infallible, untouchable, eulogised, their work evaluated largely by focusing on the speed of turnaround and assessment outcomes. The risk with this approach? We grow blind to what is hardest to measure: values, educational principles, culture and climate. With an overemphasis on crude assessment data, we sometimes ignore the true stories of sustainable school improvement. At least five of Mr Gove's lauded headteachers have been suspended from their roles, such are the perils of hubris in a high-stakes Wild West where data rules.

What should be done

When we consider how assessment could be used to impact on learning actions and behaviours, there is much that we can learn from Atul Gawande's pioneering work as a surgeon and consultant leader. In *The Checklist Manifesto* (2009, p.102), he maintains that thinking of surgery in terms of teamwork is more likely to produce positive results than the cult of 'the surgeon as virtuoso, like a concert pianist'. This chimes with Dylan Wiliam's concept of 'responsive teaching', in which the climate for learning elicits co-ownership of learning between teachers, pupils and learning communities. High-quality assessment necessitates a relationship between prior learning, intended learning, pupils and adults. Assessment is inextricable from responsive teaching; the quality of one is dependent on the other. Assessment is primarily a process whereby teacher and student find out what the pupils know and can do, and how they can take their next steps in learning.

With responsive teaching, deep learning flourishes because teachers create fail-safe spaces in classrooms where pupils have time to discuss ideas, check for meaning and receive multiple models of learning responses to help them build a strong identity with learning content. These are classrooms where practice and reflection are modelled to the highest quality, helping pupils to develop confidence. Responsive teaching ensures that mistakes are valued as new learning opportunities. This helps teachers to better assess who has acquired certain levels of knowledge, meaning that they are better equipped to support pupils in building new learning. Expert teachers are good at identifying what type of practice pupils might benefit from. They are supportive of risk-taking and encourage children to take on more challenging tasks. They have a growth mindset; they understand that people need to learn from mistakes in order to grow. In a responsive learning environment, the whole community fundamentally understands that someone's current position is not necessarily a predictor of their future achievement; they believe that people need to be able to grow in a role to have the right opportunity.

In Gawande's *Being Mortal* (2015, p. 229), he explores the marginal status between terminal illness and death and how the medical profession has got it wrong in its provision for those at the end of their lives. He argues powerfully that medicine's focus is too narrow, leaning too far towards repair, safety and protection. By contrast, *Being Mortal* provides examples where 'living for the best possible day instead of sacrificing time now for time later' is helping terminally ill patients the world over make life-altering decisions about living better. Central to his argument, Gawande cites research, including his own recorded interviews with patients. He specifies that contrary to what we might think, human beings are hardwired and driven by our overwhelming desire to seek a bigger cause in life – this transcends ourselves and is rooted in our need to make a difference. In an education context, expansive assessment is fundamentally about helping learners connect learning from their starting points to a learning goal that has substance, meaning and purpose. It is expansive because it gives ownership to pupils but it also connects with pedagogy and curriculum so that learning has a direction of travel. It has possibilities.

Being Mortal provides a complex but compelling narrative about what we value most when faced with our ultimate challenges. This includes an emotional testimony from Gawande himself, when faced with his own father's terminal decline. Our 'transcendent desire' does not necessarily produce happiness per se, and can even be painful. He highlights how we all desire something more than immediate pleasures. From the elderly patients who find renewed purpose in caring for plants and animals, to the cancer patient who gains renewed strength from teaching her pupils music, the message is clear: human potential is located beyond immediate gain. What we learn is that the desire to belong, find purpose and help others achieve their potential provides the most powerful medicine for both patients and carers. The human spirit's ability to transcend self-desire has so much more potential to heal than we ever realised, and on multiple levels. Viewed in this way, expansive assessment has the capacity to connect learning from error with making a difference for oneself and for others. The motivation to learn from our mistakes exceeds possibilities when it has purpose and meaning. Expansive assessment and expansive curriculum are two sides of the same coin.

So what does this look like in practice? The most expansive forms of assessment are integrally linked to helping pupils to make better progress, rather than simply reporting standards. For too long, the standards agenda has created a culture of compliance whereby summative and formative assessment feed accountability, instead of growing new learning. For example:

- Written marking, typically, has been overvalued as a teaching device, where its use is largely a demonstration to external bodies of policy compliance than it is to support pupil learning.
- The language of feedback has evolved from a vacuous, meaningless set of statements or grades (e.g. 'good effort') to generic wish statements that children cannot possibly act upon without a deeper level of interaction with others or direct teaching of a skill. Again, the approach is based on the need to satisfy an external machine that requires compliance to create an illusion of consistency in schools.

Expansive assessment, however, places learners at the centre, maximising the potential of collaboration and high-quality teaching to provide the right opportunities to practise skills in a meaningful context. This approach requires the cultivation of high trust and a symbiotic relationship between planning, assessment and evaluation. It also relies upon high-quality collective dialogue about learning, feeding curiosity and nurturing resilience. If Atul Gawande describes how the best surgeons tune in to the needs and context of their patients, in order to find a solution to a medical problem, so too do the most effective teachers guide learners in making better choices about their next learning steps (see Table 13 below).

Table 13 Different types of relationships have different impacts on learners

Paternalistic relationships	Informative relationships	Interpretive relationships
Provides the answers	Presents facts and knowledge for others to make choices	Tunes in to the context by asking questions
Believes experts know best	Obsessive about detail	Looks for patterns and relationships
Makes the critical decisions associated with learning	Can overwhelm with too much information but doesn't take responsibility	Guides learning towards best outcome
Takes control of learning	Takes least control of learning	Seeks shared responsibility
Impact: Learner has low levels of autonomy.	Impact: Learner is confused.	Impact: Learner feels empowered.

The language of assessment

At Woodhill and Foxfield schools, what helped pupils take greater responsibility for their own learning was creating a common language of assessment. It gave pupils a voice to articulate their thinking, helping them to reframe the narrative of 'real' learning away from facile, opaque task responses (e.g. 'I need to do more of…') towards a more ambitious repertoire of growth-centred feedback. Across age phases, pupils and staff have crafted a collective set of expectations whereby pupils are able to consider, reflect, respond and challenge from different perspectives.

The sentence stems in Table 14 not only expand the possibilities for pupils to deepen learning, but they also grow pupils' confidence, helping them to create an internal representation for learning and a vocabulary to evidence progress. Feedback prompts like the ones below are intrinsically reliant on dialogue, discussion and social learning. They ensure that we get inside pupils' heads to better understand their thinking.

Feedback prompts

What else do you know? How?

Convince me / prove it / what's the rule? / explain your thinking…

Always, sometimes, never true?

Can you find?

What's the same, what's different?

Complete the pattern / continue the pattern

Can you argue against rather than for?

Spot the mistake / which is correct? Why?

True or false? How do you know?

What comes next?

Do, then explain

Make up an example / write more statements / create a question

Possible answers / other possibilities

What do you notice?

This supports both pupils and teachers in what Ron Berger (2003, p. 103) describes as 'turning up the knob that regulates quality and effort. Is this good enough? Does it meet my standards? Changing assessment at this level should be the most important goal of school.' This type of feedback also forces pupils to deliberately slow down and makes them more reflective. Responses require more care, consideration and reflection. This helps the learner appreciate that the quality of feedback response is more valuable than the speed of task-completion; learning becomes more about the rehearsal than the performance.

Provocative prompts

We can also break down the type of feedback we provide pupils into different areas. Table 15 shows feedback prompts defined by area. It is the provocative prompt that is more likely to help pupils deepen reflection and reasoning linked to learning tasks, and therefore extend meaning.

Table 14 Thinking and reasoning sentence stems help to deepen pupils' learning

_____thinks that_____. Do you agree? Explain your answer.	I think… I agree because I know that… I disagree because I know that… If you… For example, … To explain, … To prove this, you only have to…
_____thinks_____; however,_____ thinks_____. Could you convince the person who is wrong that they are wrong?	I know you are wrong because… Your answer is incorrect because… You have… whereas you should have… A better way might have been to… A more effective method would be to…
Can you explain the rule for…	The rule is… The pattern I used is… To find the next number you have to…
Can you prove the following statements: E.g. Odd + odd = even Odd + even = odd Even + even = even	I can prove this by… To prove this, you have to… This demonstrates that… This clearly shows that…
If you fold a [shape] into a [fraction] you will always get a [____]. Is this correct?	The statement is_____because_____ If you_____ To demonstrate this you need to This proves that You can therefore conclude that_____
Which number is the odd one out?	_____is the odd one out because_____
Do you agree with this calculation?	The calculation is_____because_____ To correct this, they would need to_____
Which of these statements is true?	I think _____is _____ because____ I can prove this by_____ I can demonstrate this by_____ This shows that_____
Would you rather have [fraction] of a _____or [fraction]?	I would rather have _____ because____ To illustrate this I can To demonstrate this I can_____ I can show this by _____
Teach your partner to_	To do this you have to_____ First you have to_____ Next_____ Finally_____
Why are these number sentences the same total?	The number sentences have the same total because…

Table 15 Types of feedback can be classified, with provocative prompts more likely to help pupils develop reasoning

Feedback prompts	Actions
Pre-emptive (pre-assessment)	Teach rather than wait to give feedback on predictable failure
Example prompt (corrective)	Clarify what pupils are attempting to learn by providing concrete examples: 'Here are two ways to do this…'
Scaffolding response (process)	Pupils still struggling with concepts/skills are given more structure: 'Which specific language features are missing?'
Reminding prompt (self-regulation)	When learning is 'almost there' and learners need to remember to use it: 'Remember that the conclusion needs to link back to the opening paragraph'
Provocative prompt (self-regulation)	When learners have met success criteria, they are encouraged to think further (reasoning): 'How would you argue against this rather than for it?'

Too often, teacher feedback focuses on reminding prompts, which are, most commonly, linked to procedural fluency rather than extending meaning. Reminding prompts are slaves to accountability because they are written as much for the adults who monitor books and scrutinise pupil progress as they are written for pupils. Reminding prompts give the important message that teachers are aware of 'errors' and conscious of standards. They seldom extend meaning or challenge learners to engage with the learning content on a deeper level.

By contrast, the provocative feedback prompt encourages pupils to take ownership of their learning and to justify viewpoints. Provocative feedback prompts impact most deeply when pupils have formed a strong bond with the learning material through curriculum experience. They help to amend the message that learning is not rapid, but slow and complex – that learning necessitates deliberate practice and reworking of ideas. Implicitly, they also provides pupils with a script that learning is not completed until it achieves excellence. It thrives on communication and feedback; it promotes a growth mindset. Here are some examples.

1 Refining thinking (Photos 18 and 19)

Sometimes, we need to be explicit about expectations and challenge pupils to refine their language and expression. This is an essential part of the mastery journey towards excellence. The focus with these examples is less about the evaluation of learning and more about the need to demonstrate a greater degree of control as a writer. The questioning provides a scaffold for deeper learning.

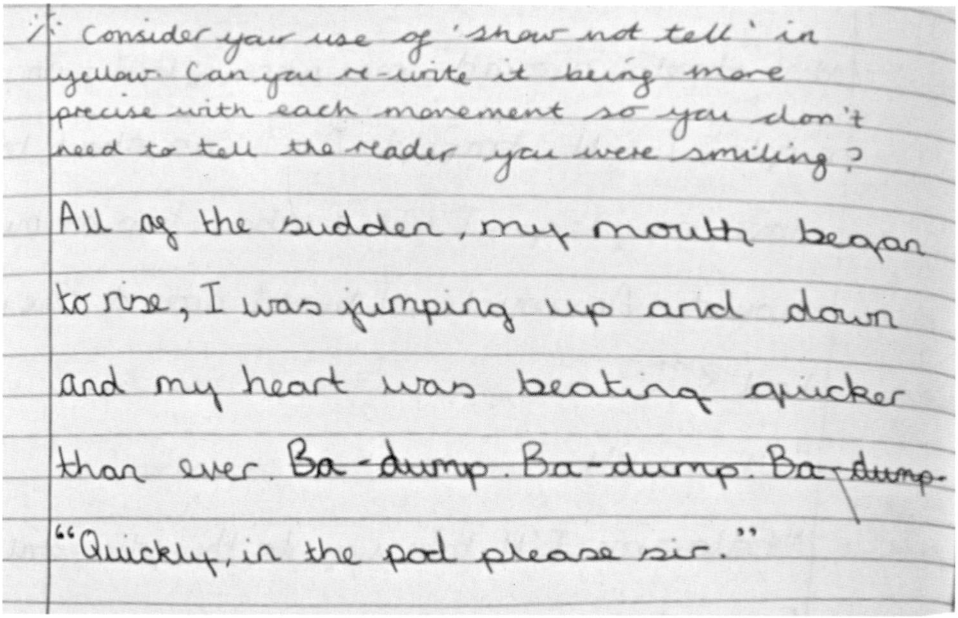

? Consider your use of 'show not tell' in yellow. Can you re-write it being more precise with each movement so you don't need to tell the reader you were smiling?

All of the sudden, my mouth began to rise, I was jumping up and down and my heart was beating quicker than ever. Ba-dump. Ba-dump. Ba-dump. "Quickly, in the pod please sir."

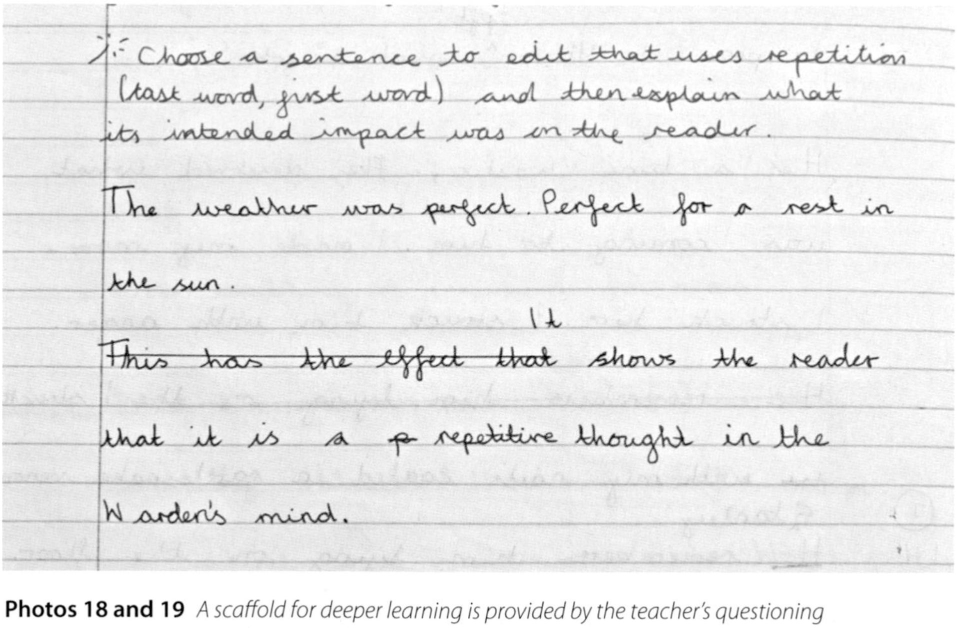

? Choose a sentence to edit that uses repetition (last word, first word) and then explain what its intended impact was on the reader.

The weather was perfect. Perfect for a rest in the sun.

It
This ~~has the effect that~~ shows the reader that it is a ~~p~~ repetitive thought in the Warden's mind.

Photos 18 and 19 *A scaffold for deeper learning is provided by the teacher's questioning*

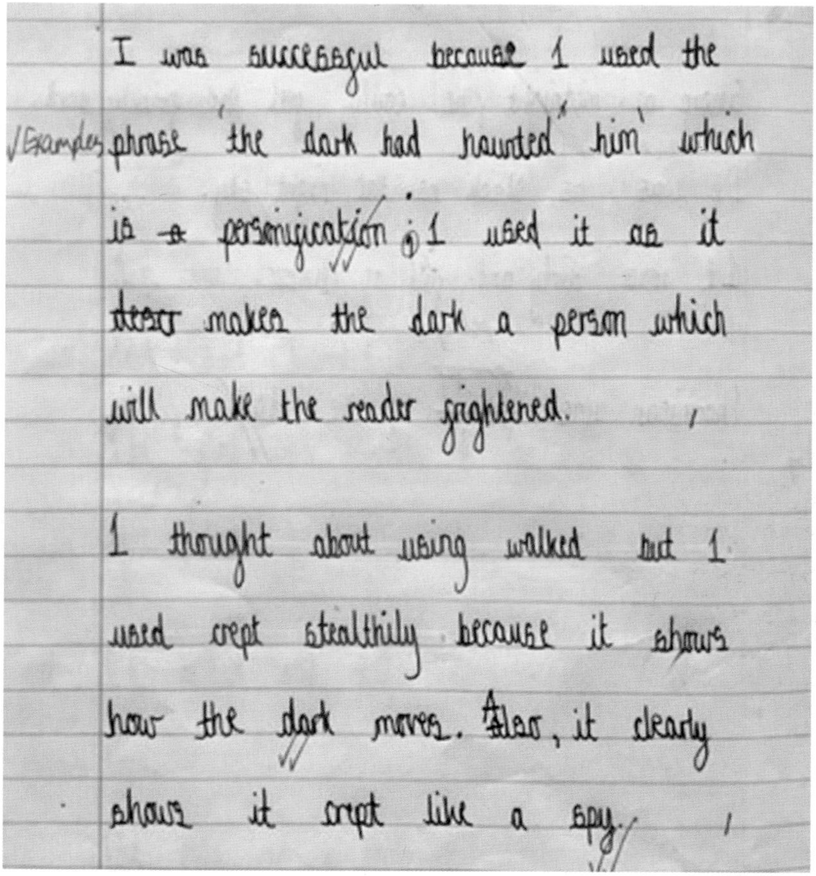

I was successful because I used the phrase 'the dark had haunted him' which is a personification. I used it as it makes the dark a person which will make the reader frightened.

I thought about using walked but I used crept stealthily because it shows how the dark moves. Also, it clearly shows it crept like a spy.

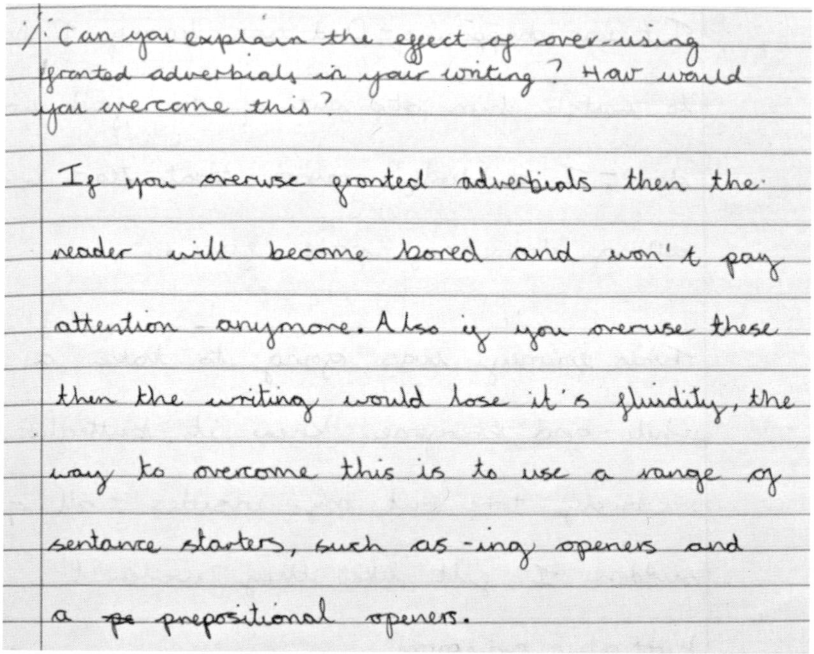

Can you explain the effect of over-using fronted adverbials in your writing? How would you overcome this?

If you overuse fronted adverbials then the reader will become bored and won't pay attention anymore. Also if you overuse these then the writing would lose it's fluidity, the way to overcome this is to use a range of sentence starters, such as -ing openers and a prepositional openers.

Photos 20 and 21 *Pupils are asked to justify their perspectives, helping them to evaluate their learning*

> **/**: Why did you choose to use inverted commas around 'Mr' Sir? What was the intended impact?
>
> It shows the reader that he is not behaving
>
> Ⓘ
>
> LH the way a 'real' man should. It also shows sarcasm

> **/**: Choose a sentence from your writing and explain what your intended impact on the reader was.
>
> My intended impact for the sentence 'Home is all I think about.' is that I wanted the reader to know that Tara is thinking about her childhood without actually saying it to them.

Photos 22 and 23 *Feedback focused on its intended impact supports pupils' development of self-efficacy*

2 Challenging perspectives or justifying viewpoints (Photos 20 and 21)

Nothing helps us evaluate our learning better than justifying our perspective about learning. This ensures that the writer views the world through the eye of the reader and elicits a deeper level of reflection.

3 Evaluation and reflection

The quality of self- and peer-review is dependent on the quality of questioning (verbal and written). To encourage a deeper level of thinking from pupils, we need to first ensure that we are asking the right questions. If learning is a social experience, the role we play as teachers in the facilitation of deep learning is to elicit a deeper sense of thinking and reflection. Our challenge through questioning becomes internalised by pupils over time. We are modelling the learning thought processes that we hope will become positive learning dispositions. Photos 22 and 23 offer some examples of self-reflection driven by some great questioning.

Pupils evaluating learning

One way to develop a more expansive approach to assessment is to place greater emphasis on how we involve pupils in evaluating their own learning over time, and how our pupils' books can provide a rich evidence base for evaluating progress. Table 16 shows a framework for helping pupils capture evidence about their learning successes over time.

Table 16 A learning evaluation scaffold can help pupils to capture evidence of their learning successes

Key area	Strengths and examples	What I can do better
In which ways has my presentation improved? • Writing learning intentions. • Remembering dates. • Use of cursive handwriting. • Using rulers, etc.		
How have I shown greater resilience in my learning? • Increased the number of words in my writing depending on the task. • Evidence of not giving up and finishing tasks/problems. • Showing thinking in learning.		
How has feedback helped me learn better? • Have I responded to feedback? • Can I find examples of how the feedback was acted upon? • Feedback shows thinking.		
Do my books show basic learning skills are improved? • Examples of things I can do better now than I could before. • Evidence of better spelling, grammar and punctuation. • Examples of skills taught that I can now apply in learning.		
Do my books show the 'journey' of my learning? • Can I find examples where my learning in literacy links to learning in other subjects? • Am I using words and vocabulary modelled by adults in my learning? • Can I show how I am using calculation methods to solve problems?		
Which words and phrases do I now use in my writing that I didn't understand before?		
My summary thoughts about the progress in my books are…	I am most proud of…	I need to get better at…

Evidence of progress

One of the saddest things to see is so little regard being given to the learning environment or the quality of learning evidenced in books. It is our best and most reliable evidence base. With specific reference to the evidence of learning captured in pupils' books, outlined here are some of the key features I would look for as evidence that children are getting the best possible deal and making great progress.

1   Pupil books communicate school values

What children commit to speaking, writing, drawing or sharing is special and important. How we value this communicates powerful messages about our learning community. There needs to be a balance between encouraging risk-taking and mistake-making while also reinforcing the ethic of excellence that 'if it isn't perfect, it isn't finished'.

Key questions:

- Is presentation of learning valued in books?
- Do adults and children take pride in what goes into the books?
- Are expectations consistently high, taking into account learners' needs and starting points?

2   Learning journeys should be co-constructed with pupils

I don't mean feedback marking per se but, more explicitly, the relationship between learners and teachers, specifically captured and valued as important in books.

Key questions:

- Are pupils really involved in owning responsibility for their learning?
- Is there evidence in books of a learning dialogue between adults and pupils?

3   Books provide evidence of 'incidental', ongoing learning, leading to quality

Capturing the *learning journey* is critical. It provides evidence that the road map for progress and meaning-making is designed in advance, planned with quality outcomes in mind and referencing the need for 'extended abstract' thinking. The emphasis within the incidental learning should be on the quality of language, its link to the purpose and audience for learning and the challenge within the task.

Key questions:

- How engaged are pupils in reflecting on their 'useful learning mistakes'?
- Can pupils articulate their next steps?
- Can I see the narrative of the learning journey contained in books?

4 It's not the feedback but its impact that matters

If this is happening consistently and well then the evidence will clearly be visible in books.
Key questions:

- Is feedback (oral and verbal) impacting on learning?
- Is there evidence that children have responded to feedback and then done something with the feedback to make a difference in their own learning?

5 Learning should be purposeful and make connections with the world

Learning evidence in books needs to communicate that learning is important and has a purpose beyond the life of a single lesson. Photographic evidence is a good way to capture a sense of purpose when connecting drama and oral communication with learning. Ensuring that the learning context is rich and linked to the real world is another.
Key questions:

- Can pupils evidence the impact of their learning on themselves and others?
- Can pupils make links between their learning in school and its application beyond school?
- Can pupils describe what they have learnt from others and its impact?

6 Displays provide the setting for quality: they model and capture examples of excellence from books

Building on the 'ethic of excellence' theme, when pupils' books capture the evidence of a quality planned learning journey, it isn't just seen in books – it's everywhere. You can see it in the adult modelling, learning walls and, of course, pupil outcomes on display.
Key questions:

- How are learning outcomes celebrated across the curriculum?
- Do learning displays also capture evidence of the impact of learning, e.g. the evaluation of learning?
- How does published learning capture and celebrate high quality?

What gets measured in teaching gets treasured. This encourages schools to game the system and increases dependency on test-based school improvement, instead of cultivating a deep approach to learning where the needs of every single child are met. We have argued throughout this chapter that the best forms of assessment are used as a teaching tool rather than an accountability tool. Critical to the debate is that investment in expansive assessment, which includes:

- deepening pupil engagement in peer- and self-assessment
- giving pupils a language to evaluate their learning
- focusing assessment strategies on growth and progress rather than outcomes.

Expansive assessment can and does raise standards. It helps pupils to develop self-efficacy, reframes success so that pupils see their learning needs and keeps the teaching focus on improving outcomes instead of proving outcomes.

This does not mean to say that we should lower the bar in terms of teacher expectations for pupils – quite the opposite. We want our teachers to be experts in meeting the needs for every child. An expansive approach to assessment ensures that teachers know their pupils better, build stronger relationships and are able to meet their needs within the mainstream setting of a classroom. The benefits are pupils who demonstrate more positive attitudes towards learning and are able to connect learning skills beyond school, and critically, expansive assessment creates a school climate where we are much better able to celebrate individual successes.

The most enduring school improvement starts from the classroom level and is practitioner-driven, not policy-led. Analytical, academic or prescriptive leadership often fails in the most complex organisations. By contrast, learning-centred leadership, which we examine in the next chapter, creates cultural alignment, allowing change to seep into every aspect of practice, becoming part of the organisational DNA and regulating 'how we do things around here'. It is how the best schools ensure that they continuously remain at the top. It maximises social and cultural capital by concentrating on:

- **Self learning**: complete personal ownership and fidelity to *be* a learner.
- **Classroom learning**: a commitment to modelling common practices within the classroom at all times.
- **Professional learning**: developing a theory of learning for staff as well as pupils, maximising collaboration and distributing learning between classrooms.
- **System learning**: determination to ensure that learning occurs between schools and across the system.

9 Leadership and professional development

When you read the damning Foxfield Ofsted inspection report from 2014, many of the recommendations focus on strengthening accountability and an instructional approach to school improvement. For example:

1   Establishing robust procedures for checking on staff performance and holding all to account for pupils' achievements.

2   Ensuring that all staff are ambitious for pupils' achievements, and work is set at the right level to provide a suitable level of challenge for all pupils.

3   Making sure that teachers make better checks on pupils' progress and understanding in lessons.

None of the key issues were especially controversial or contested and neither was the report untypical for a school just placed into the category of inadequate. As we've discussed, our strategy for school improvement that grew out of the inspection was almost entirely reliant on strengthening collaboration between teachers and maximising the potential of teamwork. However, the words 'collaboration' or 'partnership', in any derivative, did not appear as a recommendation in the inspection report a single time.

If it is true that learning is inherently a social process, would it not also follow that, as a school community, improvement is equally dependent on working together? That when learning is social, we unlock our own and each other's creativity, are motivated because great work is done together and grow stronger because of the interdependence we have on each other's ideas, generously shared and valued?

The narrative of school improvement is one where strategy, pace-setting and robust accountability are heralded. Individualism in school leadership is celebrated, perhaps more now than ever. In the past five years, there has been a conscious effort to reward those individuals most credited for turning around failing schools – large salaries, public recognition and almost celebrity status through social media. The VIP school leader has arrived: the stories of superhero headteachers have become folklore. So too, in the past year, however, have the newspaper headlines charting their rise and fall.

Leadership styles

The reality of how schools really improve, however, is much less romantic. The Harvard Business Review published an article in March 2017. The report stated boldly that one kind of leadership, in particular, could turn around a failing school, and contrasted this with the types of leadership most likely to be celebrated. In a study of 411 school leaders in the UK, they argued that we are appointing, rewarding and recognising the wrong kind of leadership. They placed school leaders into five different categories, but found only one type that was enduring. The most effective leaders were 'least well-known, least rewarded, and least recognized' (Hill et al., 2017). The groups consisted of:

- Accountant leaders: The accountant leaders were described as most likely to grow their schools out of trouble. They are resourceful, systematic and revenue-focused. They believe that schools get into difficulty because they are small and weak. They are most likely to focus on data as the dominant indicator of success.

- Philosopher leaders: The philosopher leaders are those leaders most passionate about teaching and learning, rooted in pedagogy, but least likely to build sustainable leadership.

- Solider leaders: Soldier leaders trim and tighten, focusing on accountability. They believe in working harder and value individualism.

- Surgeon leaders: The surgeon leaders are decisive and believe in competition and winning. They are most likely to have a reputation for rapid turnaround. They believe that their job is to get a school back in shape fast, through rules and a strong work ethic.

It is these leadership traits that are most likely to be noticed and rewarded. The report highlights that we honour the surgeons for their ability to increase exam results, even though these leaders are most likely to exclude pupils or overspend on budgets. The philosophers are most likely to receive public recognition in the form of an honour from the Queen, even though they were the worst-performing leaders in the study. By contrast, there are:

- Architect leaders: Architect leaders are those who redesign school improvement through collaboration and a focus on community, and who go largely unnoticed.

The characteristics of the architect leaders are much more complex to evaluate within a model of school improvement where accountability is so closely linked to immediate impact on standards. The architects were described as those most insightful, humble and visionary. They are most likely to focus on community needs and view school improvement holistically. They combine the best parts of other leadership but have the strongest commitment to long-term success and moral purpose. The report described them as: 'stewards, rather than leaders, who are more concerned with the legacy they leave than how things look while they're there.' (Hill et al., 2017)

Critically, the report highlights our need to find and develop more school leadership architects. They question short-term measures of success and an overemphasis on achievement grades. They recognise the need to assess:

'A leader's social and economic impact both during and after their tenure using new measures…. the Architects would be highlighted as the transformational leaders they are and could then receive the recognition they deserve. As one Architect explained, "My measure of success is – are parents complaining more? And are we issuing fewer anti-social behaviour orders (ASBOs) within our local community? If so, then parents are engaging more with the school and our community is improving." Surely, this is the kind of strategic, transformational and inclusive thinking we need, if we want to actually improve results.' (Hill et al., 2017)

Architect leaders are also social leaders.

Outstanding

Foxfield Primary School was judged outstanding in September 2015, just 18 months after it was placed in special measures. Like many school success stories, the reported narrative was about relentless leadership committed to raising standards. Again, the rhetoric was far removed from the reality. Nassim Nicholas Taleb (*The Black Swan*, 2007) believes that we concentrate on things we already know and fail to take into consideration what we don't. 'Black Swans' are a little bit like architect leaders. Taleb provides a brilliant analysis of how hindsight recasts our thinking and shapes our perceptions. He highlights three key misconceptions about history distorting the reality of events:

1 The illusion of understanding – we continuously try to rationalise what is happening around us in a world that is more complex, random and unpredictable than we imagine.

2 Retrospective distortion – our predisposition to assess matters after an event (football pundit style) but then realign events to fit our view of the world.

3 Overvaluation of factual information – placing too much emphasis on the knowledge of an esteemed few rather than the reality of the majority.

Critically, Taleb argues that change happens not in sequential steps but in giant, unpredictable leaps, and that often, the unplanned events can alter courses with greater impact than those planned for. Successful schools have the knack of creating a climate where potential is released from these unplanned 'possibilities' rather than squashing them. They manage the unplanned as well as the planned. When putting together a coherent strategy, there are just too many variables in complex organisations like schools for us to predict outcomes in a 20-page document. We have to allow for failure and the unexpected.

There is also an argument that twenty-first-century system leadership is much more about learning fluidly from each other, as opposed to a linear model of plotting a carefully mapped improvement trajectory. We are more outward-facing, increasingly reliant on peer support and more comfortable in taking risks – living beyond the comfort zone. Accessing each other's learning through 'cross-fertilisation' of thinking and collaboration does not always lend itself to clean and predictable planned improvement.

Such leaders largely go unrecognised and unrewarded because they do not fit the belief system of leadership that we are fed. Taleb (2007) describes, for example, the reality of growing up in the Middle East as being very different from the reported version. Based on the way that history is reported, we are unable to truly evaluate the real story, vulnerable to the impulse to simplify, narrate and categorise, and not open enough to rewarding those who can imagine the 'impossible'.

In the case of Foxfield, the 'impossible' was a story of one school (in special measures) working entirely collaboratively with another school (in the Ofsted category of requiring improvement).

What really happened

So, what really happened?

The work of the Behavioural Insights Team in the Nudge Unit (Halpern, 2015; see p. 108) demonstrated the positive force of social attraction and influence as a means of impacting change. Social learning, however, isn't always about persuasion. Sometimes, behaviours have to change before beliefs do. Pushing and pulling are also traits of social learning – especially when those doing the pulling are peers.

When Foxfield was placed into special measures, the new leadership team had been in post for just three weeks. What we found was shocking. Organisational behaviours were centred firmly on individualism, survival and blame. There was little or no sense of togetherness and an expectation that you would be left alone unless you were being observed in a random, uncoordinated way. Schools in crisis often exhibit traits that become coping mechanisms. At Foxfield, these traits led to a cultural toxicity that stifled and disrupted the possibility of teachers learning from each other in a deep way. Gordon Stobart (2014) provides an interesting comparison between shallow and deep learning (see Table 17). The model was developed to categorise forms of learning for pupils but it works equally well within a leadership context. Schools working at crisis point often find it difficult to imagine a place beyond the shallow, which is why they are pushed even closer to the precipice of believing that tightening accountability is the only way forwards. It is easier to coerce and force change when accountability is tight. The danger within this model is that it becomes harder to see other, more expansive

Table 17 The features of shallow and deep approaches to learning can be defined (adapted from Stobart, 2014)

Approach to learning	Defining features
Surface reproducing Intention: to cope with learning requirements	**What do I need to do to survive?** Treating learning as unrelated bits of knowledge. Memorising facts and carrying out procedures routinely. Finding difficulty in making sense of new ideas. Seeking little value or meaning in either learning or tasks set. Studying without reflecting on either purpose or strategy. Feeling under pressure and worrying about learning.
Strategic reflective organising Intention: to achieve the highest possible grades	**What do I need to do to pass the tests?** Wanting to do well and achieve good grades. Motivated and organised. Putting consistent effort into studying. Managing time and effort effectively. Finding the right conditions and materials for studying. Monitoring the effectiveness of ways of studying. Being alert to assessment requirements and criteria.
Deep seeking meaning Intention: to develop ideas for yourself	**How can learning help me make better sense of the world?** Relating ideas to previous knowledge and experiences. Looking for patters and underlying principles. Checking evidence and relating it to conclusions. Examining logic and argument cautiously and critically. Becoming actively interested in learning content and forming a relationship with the learning.

possibilities, which can, in turn, lead to an overreliance on simple, instructive approaches to improvement.

Before our reforms at Foxfield and because the school was in crisis, the behaviour of self-inspection rather than group improvement was prominent. Subject leaders were busy measuring anything that moved because this was their only reference point for what they believed good leadership did. Staff exhibited random, unfocused and disconnected behaviours, which did not serve the needs of staff or children and also took up disproportionate amounts of energy. Such behaviours can have a devastating impact on the culture of a school, to the point where an openness to learning leaves a school in deep shock.

The impact of this led to teachers working in a climate of fear. Doors to classrooms were almost exclusively closed; teachers taught and planned in isolation. There was no common way of working together and no single vision for teaching and learning. Even the placement of the school leadership office gave a very strong message to the community that learning happens in silos. Staff and pupils had to enter a coded number simply to get through to speak to a senior member of staff, and the door handles were too high for most children to reach.

This fear of failure created paralysis because teachers were frightened to make mistakes and take risks. Where there was good practice, this was hidden away by individuals, too scared to share their expertise in case they were either exposed as outliers or criticised by others for daring to work differently. Simultaneously, the concept of discretionary effort came to a standstill. Teachers resented giving more than they had to because innovation was neither recognised nor valued. The culture of compliance had the negative consequence of teachers interpreting policy in a literal or obstructive way. Staff became unionised and resentful towards leadership demands to give more.

Professional development

The second negative impact of the toxic culture relates to professional development. Not only did teachers work in isolation, but they also learnt in isolation. When the Ofsted inspection team questioned the value of continuous professional development, teacher responses were unequivocal: 'This has been the worst year of my professional career.' 'There has been no support for NQTs.' The final published inspection report confirmed this:

> 'Staff, especially those new to teaching, have received too little training to help them to enhance pupils' progress. Not all have the skills to: manage pupils' behaviour well; promote effective learning in English and mathematics; or help children in Reception and Nursery make the best possible start to their education.' (Ofsted, 2014)

These were typical responses and expose another fault line in the 'accountability-works' model for school improvement. Because the school, prior to inspection, had focused solely on tightening accountability, it had become even more isolationist, inward-looking and constrictive. Professional development became instructional, used as a coping mechanism, rather than expansive. The more leadership tried to provide clarity and build a common expectation, the more narrow it felt to work in these conditions. What the school had failed to understand was that the school required a bilingual and bicultural approach to improvement – leadership adept enough to operate multi-dimensionally. Instruction alone was never going to work. Ironically, just as Joshua Cooper Ramo describes in *The Seventh Sense* (2016, p. 61), if we are to define our own future when faced with adversity, 'it means not running away, but running at terrifying forces'. In the case of Foxfield, on the tipping point of an inadequate inspection judgement, the best thing for the school would have been to strengthen collaboration to build a more positive culture and climate – which was exactly what we did.

The strategy, then, if there was one at that point, was to alter behaviours of teachers so that staff were forced to work more closely together and align actions with a belief system framed around core values. We knew that the policy of 'behaviour change first, cultural change later' would have a limited lifespan but we also hoped that if we stuck closely to changing behaviours, beliefs would evolve over a longer period and that the positive behaviours would build a more collaborative approach to learning.

- The first thing we did was purchase door stops for every single classroom to make it impossible for teachers to work in isolation.
- The second action was to remove the keypad locks on doors to the leadership office so that pupils and staff could access senior staff when they needed to.
- The third action, which followed quickly from the first two, was to move the entire leadership office away from the front of the school (which was less accessible) right into the centre and heart of where children's learning was taking place.

We then embarked on a journey to support staff in working more collaboratively in a positive and affirming way. This took three forms:

1 We removed the structure of teachers planning learning units in isolated year groups and created a whole-school topic linked to the heritage of London and the Royal Arsenal.

2 Teachers planned together between schools so that each phase team had support in designing and developing meaningful learning units.

3 We engineered a practitioner-devised framework for evaluating teaching and learning, which was developed and implemented in a collaborative way.

What we had managed to design was, in effect, a collaborative model for school improvement that placed teachers at the heart of their own learning journey. The impact was stunning.

The aim was to improve the quality of teaching using a more rounded, developmental approach that enables teachers to self-evaluate the impact of teaching against agreed standards and work collaboratively to improve teaching. We created a programme for staff that involved training teachers to engage in a shared approach to improving teaching. Every teacher and leader was assigned a role as either coach, mentor or mentee. Alongside this, we devised a common set of standards (linked neatly with the teacher standards), aligned to the core aspects of practice that we collectively agreed would have the biggest impact on raising expectations in the classroom. Within these, we generated a new form of language that meant that nobody was judged or labelled as a failure. Everyone started from somewhere, so our key descriptors ran from *emerging* through to *embedded excellence*. The idea was that all teachers have their own pathway to achieving lead practitioner status within all or some aspects of practice at our school, so that we could then acknowledge how together we might grow our leadership pipeline. An example of our framework is shared in Table 18, p.148.

Table 18 Progress can be mapped from emerging through to embedded excellence

	Emerging	Developing	Highly accomplished	Embedded excellence
Learning environment	The environment is organised and purposeful. Learning environments identify key areas within classrooms including book corners, learning walls, topic tables and curriculum areas. Pupil books and other resources are stored neatly in an organised way. Resources are clearly labelled.	Learning environments are stimulating, well-organised and contain evidence of high expectations. This can be identified through the organisation of resources, the quality of learning on display and through quality of modelling.	The learning environment is aspirational, with every area providing models of excellence. Key vocabulary, examples of modelling and learning walls reflect the highest expectations and are used by pupils to enhance learning.	The learning environment is an inspirational place to learn. There is multiple evidence that the environment is used as a resource to enhance learning, build collaboration and promote the school's values.
Expectations across curriculum	Learning experiences across the curriculum are planned for using school formats and are linked to age-related expectations. These are connected using a mid-term planning framework. Links with the community, including trips and visits are planned for.	Learning across subjects is linked to a rich context that develops skills linked to national curriculum expectations. Curriculum expectations are matched to pupils' needs, which are reflected in topic choices, differentiation and quality of outcomes in books.	Curriculum expectations are high in all subjects across the curriculum. Pupils' books provide evidence of a pride in learning and capture a learning journey. Learning experiences often enable pupils to engage in problem-solving or link learning to the real world.	The highest expectations for all curriculum areas enable all pupil groups to make the best possible progress. Pupils are involved in making choices about their learning, which is personalised to meet specific needs. Pupils co-construct learning experiences and use the curriculum to make a positive impact beyond school.

Feedback marking / Assesment for learning (AfL)	Written feedback is provided in core subjects weekly. Books provide evidence of pupil responses. Mini plenaries, talk for learning and opportunities for reflection on learning are planned for. Some questioning is used to evaluate learning.	Assessment and feedback is effective in reading, writing or maths and supports pupils in knowing what they need to do in order to make progress. Lessons contain opportunities for reflection, discussion and learning review. Mini plenaries are planned for to support evaluation of learning. Some pupils are clear about next learning steps and can share these when asked.	Pupils respond well to regular written feedback, with evidence that this is enhancing learning. Feedback enables most pupils to develop basic skills, leading to good progress. Most pupils can identify next learning steps and are clear about how feedback supports future learning. Systems for enabling pupils to evaluate learning are embedded and applied consistently.	Pupils benefit from consistently high-quality assessment and constructive feedback, much of which is exceptionally good and leads to excellent progress in lessons. Checking for understanding is an embedded feature of learning. Pupils are fully involved in evaluating their own and each other's learning and use a common language for AfL to excellent effect.
Adult modelling	Adult modelling is evident in lessons and in planning. Modelling is linked to curriculum planning and intended learning. Learning displays meet school expectations.	Modelling reflects class learning needs and contains high expectations. Modelling is interactive and involves pupils through good questioning and use of adults. There is good evidence to support how modelling impacts on learning. The displayed modelling captures the learning journey over time.	Modelling precisely meets the needs of learners and bridges the gap between what they already know and can do with support. Modelling is co-constructed with pupils and enables rich dialogue about learning and metacognition. Pupil modelling and modelling by other adults is a common feature of lesson structure.	High quality modelling is an embedded feature of practice. Pupils can describe how modelling scaffolds learning and the impact on progress. All pupils can demonstrate how modelling enables extended learning. Modelling leads to enhanced independence, collaboration and pupils' ability to evaluate learning successes.

Table 18 (continued)

	Emerging	Developing	Highly accomplished	Embedded excellence
Questioning for understanding	Key questions are evident in weekly planning. These are sometimes differentiated and targeted at specific pupils' needs. Questioning sometimes moves beyond information recall or knowledge recall.	Teaching uses questioning purposefully to check for understanding and challenge learners. Open-ended questions are planned for and differentiated for specific pupil groups. Learning tasks build on planned enquiry questions.	Questioning is used adaptively to enhance quality learning experiences. Typically, questioning enables learners to engage in dialogic talk and collaboration. Pupils are comfortable with being challenged and engage in purposeful talk for learning. There is evidence of questioning enabling pupils to extend learning.	Questioning is an embedded and core feature of teaching sequences. Pupils and adults use questioning to co-construct learning, which promotes high-quality learning experiences. Pupil books and the learning environment provide excellent evidence of questioning, enabling accelerated progress. Questioning strategies are used equally well amongst all pupil groups and learning needs.
Collaborative learning	Planning identifies opportunities for collaboration in learning. This is evidenced in the use of talk partners and group discussion in lessons.	There is a clear learning journey over time but the quality of outcomes is inconsistent. Some pupils are challenged while others are not, leading to inconsistent progress over time.	There is clear evidence in books that learning connects skills over time, with opportunities to apply learning and produce quality learning. Learning journeys are differentiated to meet individuals' needs, resulting in good progress.	Evidence in books for all pupils provides evidence that planning is ambitious and deeply connected over time and across subjects. Pupils have multiple opportunities to apply skills in new and exciting ways.
Problem-solving	Planning identifies opportunities for pupils to engage in problem-solving. Problem-solving strategies are modelled during lessons.	Planning and feedback marking provide opportunities for pupils to extend learning through problem-solving. Typically, this is through an extension task or linked to a planned problem-solving activity. Learning tasks provide opportunities to apply skills taught to problem-solving.	Problem-solving is established in planning and evidenced consistently in pupils' books. Pupils demonstrate good problem-solving skills and collaborate well to work through problems systematically. Pupils are able to explain strategies and thinking when problem-solving – as evidenced in pupil books and discussion.	Pupils are not only skilled in solving problems but are active in seeking opportunities to link problem-solving to real life. There are excellent curriculum opportunities to use a range of skills in new contexts. Pupils demonstrate independence and a desire to plan their own problem-solving linked to life beyond school.

Challenge in lessons	Differentiation is planned for with learning intentions matched to pupils' levels of achievement and assessments.	Through high expectations and planned questioning, challenge is matched appropriately to pupils' learning needs. This is evidenced in the quality of differentiation and progression in pupils' books. As a result, some pupil groups make good progress.	Teaching systematically builds on prior skills and challenges all pupil groups. Teaching effectively bridges the gap between the known and unknown, often providing imaginative and fun opportunities to extend learning through challenging expectations. Through high-quality modelling and scaffolding, pupil groups are well supported.	Expectations are consistently high. There is a shared culture and expectation that learning is engaging and challenging. Pupils respond positively to high-quality teaching, with evidence that this leads to pupils engaging in a range of investigation opportunities. Lessons contain embedded systems to encourage debate and discussion amongst pupils.
Support & intervention	Other adults are identified in planning, including how they support learning. Interventions and specific programmes for learning are evident in lessons.	Other adults provide good value and ensure lessons flow well. Adult intervention is matched well to pupils' learning needs. Adults are aware of pupil next steps and ensure pupils are engaged in learning.	Adults are able to model well and share the same high expectations for pupil learning as class teachers. Adults are deployed to support a range of pupils, including more able. Other adults model expectations well, leading to supported pupils making good progress.	Expectations are consistently high for all pupils amongst adults. Within the classroom, there is a shared responsibility that all pupils will make excellent progress. Relationships amongst adults, team teaching, delivery of specialist interventions and planned support lead to all pupils making excellent progress.

As well as generating a kinder way to evaluate our work, which ensured that staff were at the centre of its implementation, we plotted the marginal gains that we believed would have the biggest immediate impact on developing relationships and trust across the school community. These gains were our quick wins to provide the biggest possible message that the school was changing for the better. They covered social routines and rituals for meeting and greeting families, arrangements for lunchtime meal provision, digital communication through our website and routines for coach and mentor relationships. If the strategy was one to raise collective ambition across a community, the narrative was that community matters.

The quality of teaching improved dramatically, within a time period of just one term. Many of those implementing improvement were teachers written off just weeks earlier as failing children. When we evaluated what had made the biggest difference to their practice, collaboration with others and between schools shone through. Staff were effusive:

- 'Observing phonics; pace and expectation: children were able to keep up with the session, enjoyed the challenge and settled quickly into the routine.'

- 'Seeing behaviour management [in another class] gave children the full responsibility for own actions, and sanctions/follow-up actions reflected this.'

- 'Observing a Year 2 lesson made me realise how much children rely on a positive role model and a pacey lesson. Also, it made me realise that my class are still very much in the KS1 mindset and the transition between KS1 and KS2 is very demanding. Therefore, they need an extremely positive teacher who can deliver lessons to make them as engaging as possible.'

- 'Observing X. Her classroom was a calm environment where children were able to access quality teaching without the need for stopping continually for low-level behaviour disruptions. Because of this the children were able to learn and access much more information and teaching, which in return will develop them better academically and socially.'

- 'Observing X. Her enthusiasm and ability to engage all children through her quick-paced and lively style of teaching. This motivated the children massively and had a positive impact on their learning.'

- 'I observed X and the pace of his lesson had a big impact on the way in which I taught my lessons after that. I have also implemented guided groups and observed my mentor to find out how to make them successful within my class. I have found that they have worked really well especially during maths where I have a group of children who benefit from a higher pitch.'

One teacher's response stood out in particular:

'Since September, I feel that my biggest success has been building relationships with the children and their parents/carers. After an NQT meeting that was followed by a PDM [staff meeting] about building relationships, I felt truly inspired. I have since made an effort to introduce a

number of new things into my classroom to improve relationships, not only between me and the children but also between the children themselves. An example of this can be something as simple as remembering the children's birthdays and greeting them every morning and afternoon at the door, or having a circle time about friendship. It is incredible to see how these small changes have made such a huge, positive difference in my classroom.'

Key questions to consider:

1 How does your school plan for effective learning-centred leadership, including professional learning, own learning, classroom learning and system learning? Are there any strengths or gaps in different aspects of learning-centred leadership?

2 How is time made for teachers to develop and embed practice in classrooms?

3 Are all senior leaders' role models for learning? Can they walk the walk as well as they talk the talk?

4 Are leaders aware of their own leadership impact? Do they bring light or shade?

5 How does leadership maximise the potential and power of collaboration amongst teams?

In the final chapter, I will draw some conclusions together, leaving us with some closing questions and recommendations for the future of our education system.

10 Conclusion

Writing this book has been a journey. It is clearer to me now than ever before that the narrative of how schools improve life chances for pupils has been portrayed incorrectly. If robust and tight system-wide accountability worked as effectively as we are told, why is it that the achievement divide between our most and least privileged communities is so great? According to the *Time for Change* social mobility report (2017), it would take decades to close. If almost 90 per cent of our schools are now judged by Ofsted to be good or better, why is it that so many of our pupils still fail to achieve a basic standard of education and why is it that, compared to other developed countries, we rank only 23rd according to PISA tables? In 2016, barely 39 per cent of pupils in receipt of the Pupil Premium reached the expected standard of basic skills in reading, writing and maths at Key Stage 2. Could it be possible that our reliance on accountability frameworks, including publishing test scores, ranking schools and exam factory approaches towards learning, contributes to the problem? And if we are open to the possibility of this, are there alternative approaches that are more aligned with trust and collaboration instead of competition? Essentially, is accountability working for all children and communities?

The prevailing narrative draws us to think of school improvement in terms of *actions* rather than *interactions*. It simplifies learning as a consequence of teaching instead of a complex sequence of useful learning mistakes, experiences and connections between people. We have blindly accepted accountability in education as a good thing, accepted that it has served us well. Frequent testing, crude inspection frameworks and an addiction to policy reform continue to dictate the tempo of education policy. The result? Lower levels of autonomy in schools and a lack of trust in teachers to use professional judgement in order to find solutions.

Our narrow focus on knowledge and intelligence has blindsided us from the genuine challenge of ensuring that young people are skilled to navigate a world of increasing complexity. Globally, we are healthier, live longer and are better educated. At the same time, 700 million people are estimated to live in extreme poverty, where, in some nations, life expectancy is less than 60. Young people believe that the world has become an unsafe place in which to live, but do want to be taught the skills to make a bigger difference. Words like 'society' and 'community' are becoming important to us once again.

Running parallel to this argument, employers are calling for education to expand its focus beyond the traditional cognitive domain, to embrace the broader skills family. This includes an increased emphasis on teamwork, resilience, creativity and mindset. An education system that has largely been built on the foundations of knowledge and intelligence is not helping to produce the 'whole-person leadership' that companies need. We have reduced learning to cause and effect, pass or fail, and continue to perpetuate the false narrative that solutions are one-dimensional rather than multi-dimensional. Intellectual performance (IQ) has delivered smarter, brainier individuals, perhaps more than our planet has ever possessed, but the benefits of improving concrete skills (cognitive domain) have not made our world a more socially responsible place. Despite the successes of democracy, freedom of speech, increased global literacy and higher proportions of young people enjoying formal education, we have still not mastered the art of critical thinking, kindness and generally taking care of each other. Afflicted by fake news, media bias, inequality and cognitive dissonance, a new age of reason calls for young people to learn to think impartially, navigate the dangers of hubris and discern between what is morally right and wrong. If we do not make this our priority, it begs the question: what is the purpose of education?

The second, perhaps bigger, risk is that failing to engage meaningfully in finding solutions pins responsibility and agency on the wrong people – passing the baton to those who are better at explaining than understanding! Bureaucrats, consultants, policymakers, politicians, inspectors – these people are better able to advise their linear solutions than understand the complexity of leading through relationships. They think in single steps, actions and obvious solutions. They value the outcome of the performance as greater than the journey of struggle. There is a danger that by not taking greater risks and responsibility for redefining what matters most in education, we continue to rely on those who have never delivered, never taught or failed and picked themselves up again, to determine the future.

A school improvement model for the future

The solutions are there in our classrooms and schools, residing in the creativity and steadfastness of teacher leaders prepared to think differently. Revolutions, after all, start in classrooms. It requires us to deepen collaboration, spread risk amongst teams and notice the incidental opportunities for change. But we need to celebrate the stories of transformation – teachers prepared to build improvement bottom-up, designers of possibility, entrepreneurs and innovators, teachers who value the network as change agents more than the establishment. The biggest gains will not be found in policies but through teachers working alongside each other, sharing expertise, developing practice through trial and error, embracing mistakes.

Just as the possibilities for pupil learning will be enhanced by deepening collaboration, problem-solving and reasoning in the classroom, so too will system-wide teaching be improved by embracing more abstract, fluid kinds of learning. People understand concepts when they are forced to think them through, to discuss them with others and to use them to solve problems. We don't spontaneously transfer what we have learned from one concrete example to another in the same abstract category. Learning depends on interaction, discourse, widening social circles and arenas of debate.

Expertise comes from the confidence to experiment, apply learning in new contexts and play creatively with learning elements – it is the organic model of improvement that we have discussed so much in this book. What separates this model from the one-dimensional option, plucked from a shelf, is that teachers become artists; they have the confidence to discover new possibilities and shape them into brilliance. If this is you, if your school cherishes these beliefs, it will indeed be a special place to learn.

Key questions to consider:

1 Do our classrooms and communal spaces reflect the values, expectations and belief in excellence that we all aspire to? Do we want to spend more time in them? Do they model what we cherish most?

2 Do our teachers have clarity about our core beliefs about the purpose of education? This includes how learning connects to the wider world and our fundamental ambitions to use education to change the world.

3 Do we have a shared teaching sequence that underpins what we do and how this maximises learning? Does it include the journey of learning as well as the specifics of teaching? Does it include pupils as teachers as well as teachers as learners?

4 Do we believe that learning is about interaction with others – a social exchange? Do we maximise the possibilities for this to shape learning in our classrooms?

5 Does assessment practice allow and encourage mistake-making? How does the language of feedback encourage pupils to deepen their learning reflections?

6 Does our school make time for deep collaboration between teachers? Does it make space for research, planned risk-taking and sharing ideas? Does it push beyond the school and spread into other schools? Is it celebrated?

7 Finally, do we care more about what our children and communities think and less about what an inspector thinks?

A school improvement model that works

When Ofsted revisited Foxfield in September 2015, everybody knew that the inspection outcome would be different. Without being overconfident, there was a sense of anticipation and excitement. So much had happened, but the fundamental key to success was that Foxfield had become a school where people came first. We had offered an alternative to leadership that was more human, kinder and more empathetic to the context of our community – and it worked.

The published report from 2015 highlighted:

'Teaching is highly effective and teachers know that only the best is good enough. The quality of their work is part of a continuous cycle of professional development. They use and link action research to the needs of the school, individuals and national priorities.

Extensive professional development has increasingly led to staff developing their particular strengths as they are equipped with appropriate skills to take on wider roles. For example, teachers at the start of their second year of teaching gained ample experience to begin shadowing the school's leadership programme.

Pupils are confident and extremely positive about their learning. They are also communicative when appropriate but exercise self-discipline very well. These characteristics support them extremely well in their learning and are evident in the way they work for long stretches and are able to make a smooth transition from one subject to the next without losing focus.

Good quality nurturing supports pupils to thrive very well at the school. Pupils understand and live the values that the school instils in them. They care for and support each other very well, showing sensitivity and understanding of their peers with special and/or medical needs. Unacceptable name calling is rare. Pupils respect each other, they show kindness and consideration towards each other.'

The keys to our success had been:

- transforming the learning environment
- creating a culture and climate of collaboration
- basing our curriculum on a combination of the three learning domains
- implementing a mastery and social learner approach to teaching and learning
- a team accountability approach with leadership
- professional development.

Education labels should never define the possibilities for schools or children. Labels have been used too readily to justify poor decision making and limit beliefs. It is not the 'disadvantaged' pupils who have a problem, it is the system which disadvantages those pupils. But we have the power to alter this narrative. We are the change makers. We are both professional and public intellectuals. When we teach, lead and interact with moral purpose, we connect our school communities with an ethical cause that has the potential to redefine the boundaries of what we thought was possible. Room by room, interaction upon interaction, the balance tilts. It necessitates we place greater faith in ourselves, rather than policy makers, to meet the global education challenges we face, so that all pupils leave our schools with the knowledge, skills and most importantly, the desire to make their mark for good. We can change the story. We are changing the story. We become the story. It starts today.

Thank you for reading this book.

References

Adams, R. (2013), "Tough and rigorous' new national curriculum published', *The Guardian*, 8 July 2013. Available at: https://www.theguardian.com/education/2013/jul/08/new-national-curriculum-published (accessed 24 April 2018).

Alexander, R. (2017), *Towards Dialogic Teaching: Rethinking Classroom Talk* (5th edn). Dialogos.

Association of Teachers and Lecturers (2015), 'Press release. Survey of NQTs.' Available at: https://www.atl.org.uk/Images/Jan%2023%20for%2027,%202015%20-%20New%20teachers%20already%20demotovated%20about%20teaching%20at%20the%20start%20of%20their%20careers.pdf (accessed 19 April 2018).

Australian Institute for Teaching and School Leadership (2016), Learning Frontiers: Insights and Ideas 2. Available at: http://ais.act.edu.au/wp-content/uploads/2016/03/insights-and-ideas-issue-2.pdf (accessed 18 April 2018).

Barber, M. (2010), The Prospects for Global Education Reform. [lecture] The College of Teachers Awards Ceremony: Biennial Lecture.

Barker, I. (2016), New analysis reveals poor families' lack of access to 'outstanding' schools. TES. Available at: https://www.tes.com/news/new-analysis-reveals-poor-families-lack-access-outstanding-schools (accessed 24 April 2018).

Berger, R. (2003), *An Ethic of Excellence: Building a Culture of Craftsmanship with Students*. Heinemann Educational Books.

Block, P. (2008), *Community: The Structure of Belonging*. Berrett-Koehler

Bloom, B. S., Krathwohl, D. R. and Masia, B. B. (1956) *Taxonomy of Educational Objectives: The Classification of Educational Goals*. New York, NY: D. McKay.

Boaler, J. (2005), The 'Psychological Prisons' from which They Never Escaped: the role of ability grouping in reproducing social class inequalities. FORUM 47(2), 135–144.

Breakspear, S. (2014), *How Does PISA Shape Education Policy Making? Why How We Measure Learning Determines What Counts in Education*. Centre for Strategic Education, Seminar Series 240. Available at: http://simonbreakspear.com/wp-content/uploads/2015/09/Breakspear-PISA-Paper.pdf (accessed 24 April 2018).

Cohen, D. (2017), 'Former gang member reveals hidden peril of knives on a walk through the streets of Woolwich', *Evening Standard*, 12 May 2017. Available at: https://www.standard.co.uk/news/crime/former-gang-member-reveals-hidden-peril-of-knives-on-a-walk-through-the-streets-of-woolwich-a3537441.html (accessed 24 April 2018).

Cooper Ramo, J. (2016), *The Seventh Sense: Power, Fortune, and Survival in the Age of Networks*. Little Brown and Company.

Coyle, D. (2010), *The Talent Code: Greatness isn't Born. It's Grown*. Arrow.

Dominiczak, P. (2013), 'Michael Gove: New curriculum will allow my children to compete with the very best', *The Telegraph*, 8 July 2013. Available at: https://www.telegraph.co.uk/education/educationnews/10166020/Michael-Gove-new-curriculum-will-allow-my-children-to-compete-with-the-very-best.html (accessed 23 April 2018).

DfE, (2016), National curriculum assessments at Key Stage 2 in England, 2016 (revised). [online]. Available at: https://assets.publishing.service.gov.uk/government/uploads/system/uploads/attachment_data/file/577296/SFR62_2016_text.pdf (accessed 18 April 2018).

DfES, 2011. The London Challenge: Transforming London Secondary Schools. Available at: http://webarchive.nationalarchives.gov.uk/20110506111425/https://www.education.gov.uk/publications/eOrderingDownload/DfES-0368-2003.pdf (accessed 23 April 2018).

Dweck, C. (2017), Mindset. Robinson.

The Economist (2010), 'An international report card: Shanghai's school students out-perform all others', 7 December 2010. Available at: https://www.economist.com/blogs/dailychart/2010/12/education (accessed 24 April 2018).

Eells, R. J. (2011), 'Meta-analysis of the relationship between collective teacher efficacy and student achievement'. PhD Dissertation, Loyola University, Chicago.

English Heritage (2012), 'Survey of London'. Available at: https://www.ucl.ac.uk/bartlett/architecture/sites/bartlett/files/48.6_st_mary_s_and_morris_walk_areas.pdf (accessed 18 April 2018).

Exley, S. (2014), 'Ofsted: New heads to be given more time to turn around under-performing schools', *TES*, 10 April 2014. Available at: https://www.tes.com/news/school-news/ofsted-watch/ofsted-new-heads-be-given-more-time-turn-around-under-performing (accessed 18 April 2018).

Floyd, T. (2016), *Dynamics of Life Expression 111*. Lulu Press.

Gawande, A. (2009), *The Checklist Manifesto: How to Get Things Right*. Metropolitan Books.

Gawande, A. (2015), *Being Mortal: Medicine and What Matters in the End*. Thorndike Press.

Goleman, D. (2013), *Focus: The Hidden Driver of Excellence*. Bloomsbury.

Greene, R. (2012), *Mastery*. Viking.

Griffith, A. and Burns, M. (2014), *Outstanding Teaching: Teaching Backwards*. Crown House Publishing.

Guskey, T. R. (2007), 'Closing Achievement Gaps: Revisiting Benjamin S. Bloom's "Learning for Mastery"'. *Journal of Advanced Academics*, 19, 8–31.

Halpern, D. (2015), *Inside the Nudge Unit: How Small Changes Can Make a Big Difference*. WH Allen.

Hattie, J. (2008), *Visible Learning: A Synthesis of Over 800 Meta-Analyses Relating to Achievement*. Routledge.

Heckman, J. (2013), *Giving Kids a Fair Chance*. MIT Press.

Hill, A., Mellon, L., Laker, B. and Goddard, J. (2017), 'The one type of leader who can turn around a failing school'. *Harvard Business Review*, updated 3 March 2017. Available at: https://hbr.org/2016/10/the-one-type-of-leader-who-can-turn-around-a-failing-school (accessed 25 April 2018).

Jones, J. (2009), The Magic Weaving Business. Leannta Publishing.

Kahneman, D. (2011), *Thinking Fast and Slow*. Farrar, Straus and Giroux.

Kime, S. et al. (2017), *What Makes Great Assessment?* Durham: Evidence Based Education.

Lepkowska, D. (2014), 'A poor Ofsted report could lead to headteachers being "disappeared"', *The Guardian*, 11 March 2014. Available at: https://www.theguardian.com/education/2014/mar/11/heads-poor-ofsted-report-dismissal-shortages (accessed 20 April 2018).

Lindstrom, M. (2016), Small Data: The Tiny Clues That Uncover Huge Trends. St Martin's Press.

Lyons, A. (2017), 'The KS2 progress data overshadows the other fantastic work of primaries', *TES*, 30 August 2017. Available at: https://www.tes.com/news/ks2-progress-data-overshadows-other-fantastic-work-primaries (accessed 24 April 2018).

MarionInstituteTV (2013), CFC Keynote – Bill Strickland: The Art of Leadership. [video] Available at: https://www.youtube.com/watch?v=1uTcb41r7LM (accessed 18 April 2018).

Marshall, P. (2013), *The Tail: How England's Schools Fail One Child in Five – and What Can be Done*. Profile Books.

Merton, R. K. (1968), The Matthew Effect in Science: The reward of communication systems of science are considered. Science, 159(3810): 56–63.

Nuthall, G. (2007), *The Hidden Lives of Learners*. NZCER Press.

OECD (2015), Japan Country Note – Results from PISA 2015. [online] Available at: http://www.oecd.org/pisa/PISA-2015-Japan.pdf (accessed 18 April 2018).

Ofsted (2013), Woodhill Primary School, School Inspection Report, 4 December 2013. Available at: https://reports.ofsted.gov.uk/inspection-reports/find-inspection-report/provider/ELS/100145 (accessed 21 April 2018).

Ofsted (2014), Foxfield Primary School, School Inspection Report, 15 May 2014. Available at: https://reports.ofsted.gov.uk/inspection-reports/find-inspection-report/provider/ELS/100156 (accessed 18 April 2017).

Ofsted (2015) Foxfield Primary School, School Inspection Report, 29 September 2015. Available at: https://reports.ofsted.gov.uk/inspection-reports/find-inspection-report/provider/ELS/100156 (accessed 24 April 2017).

Ofsted (2016) Woodhill Primary School, School Inspection Report, 12 July 2016. Available at: https://reports.ofsted.gov.uk/inspection-reports/find-inspection-report/provider/ELS/100145 (accessed 22 April 2018).

Ofsted (2018) 'School inspection handbook: Handbook for inspecting schools in England under section 5 of the Education Act 2005'. Available at: https://assets.publishing.service.gov.uk/government/uploads/system/uploads/attachment_data/file/699810/School_inspection_handbook_section_5.pdf (accessed 23 April 2018).

PwC (2016), '19th annual global CEO survey: Redefining business success in a changing world'. Available at: https://www.pwc.com/gx/en/ceo-survey/2016/landing-page/pwc-19th-annual-global-ceo-survey.pdf (accessed 23 April 2018).

PwC (2017), '20th CEO survey: 20 years inside the mind of the CEO… What's next?' Available at: https://www.pwc.com/gx/en/ceo-survey/2017/pwc-ceo-20th-survey-report-2017.pdf (accessed 23 April 2018).

Qualifications and Curriculum Authority (2007), A framework of personal, learning and thinking skills. [online]. Available at: http://webarchive.nationalarchives.gov.uk/20110215111658/http://curriculum.qcda.gov.uk/key-stages-3-and-4/skills/personal-learning-and-thinking-skills/index.aspx (accessed 18 APril 2019).

Quigley, A. (2016), *The Confident Teacher: Developing Successful Habits of Mind, Body and Pedagogy*. Routledge.

Ripley, A. (2014), *The Smartest Kids in the World*. Simon & Schuster.

Robinson, K. and Aronica, L. (2015), *Creative Schools: The Grassroots Revolution That's Transforming Education*. Viking.

Rochford Review (2016), 'The Rochford Review: Final report Review of assessment for pupils working below the standard of national curriculum tests'. Available at: https://assets. publishing.service.gov.uk/government/uploads/system/uploads/attachment_data/ file/561411/Rochford_Review_Report_v5_PFDA.pdf (accessed 21 April 2018).

RSA Action and Research Centre (2017), 'The Ideal School Exhibition'. Available at: https://www. thersa.org/globalassets/pdfs/reports/rsa-the-ideal-school-exhibition.pdf (accessed 18 April 2018).

Semuels, A. (2017), 'Japan might be what equality in education looks like', *The Atlantic*, 2 August 2017. Available at: https://www.theatlantic.com/business/archive/2017/08/japan-equal-education-school-cost/535611/ (accessed 23 April 2017).

Sinek, S. (2011), *Start With Why: How Great Leaders Inspire Everyone to Take Action*. Penguin.

Social Market Foundation (2017), Commission on Inequality in Education. [online]. Available at: http://www.smf.co.uk/wp-content/uploads/2017/07/Education-Commission-final-web-report.pdf (accessed 18 April 2018).

Social Mobility Commission (2017), 'Time for change: An assessment of government policies on social mobility 1997–2017'. Available at: https://www.gov.uk/government/uploads/system/ uploads/attachment_data/file/622214/Time_for_Change_report_-_An_assessement_of_ government_policies_on_social_mobility_1997-2017.pdf (accessed 18 April 2018).

Stobart, G. (2014), *The Expert Learner: Challenging the Myth of Ability*. Open University Press.

Strickland, B. (2007), Make the Impossible Possible. Crown Publishing Group.

Syed, M. (2011), Bounce. Fourth Estate.

Syed, M. (2015), *Black Box Thinking: The Surprising Truth About Success*. John Murray.

Taleb, N. N. (2007), *The Black Swan: The Impact of the Highly Improbable*. Random House.

Taleb, N. N. (2018), Skin in the Game: Hidden Asymmetries in Daily Life. Allen Lane.

Teaching Schools Council (2016), 'Effective primary teaching practice report 2016'. Available at: https://www.tscouncil.org.uk/resources/effective-primary-teaching-practice-2016/ (accessed 18 April 2018).

Varkey Foundation (2017), 'Generation Z: Global citizenship survey'. Available at: https://www. varkeyfoundation.org/sites/default/files/Global%20Young%20People%20Report%20 %28digital%29%20NEW%20%281%29.pdf (accessed 17 April 2018).

Wiggins, K. (2016), Scrapping the 'outstanding' grade and inspecting academy trusts: 14 key thoughts from Ofsted's next chief inspector', *Tes*. Available at: https://www.tes.com/news/ scrapping-outstanding-grade-and-inspecting-academy-trusts-14-key-thoughts-ofsteds-next-chief (accessed 24 April 2018).

Wilby, P. (2017), 'David Laws: "The quality of education policymaking is poor"', *The Guardian*, 1 August 2017. Available at: https://www.theguardian.com/education/2017/aug/01/david-laws-education-policy-schools-minister-thinktank-epi (accessed 24 April 2018).